300 Wasted Years

By
Charles Edward Scheideman

Strategic Book Publishing and Rights Co.

Strategic Book Publishing and Rights Co., LLC

USA | Singapore

www.sbpra.com

For information about special discounts for bulk purchases, please contact Strategic Book Publishing and Rights Co., LLC. Special Sales, at bookorder@sbpra.net.

ISBN: 978-1-68181-142-0

Table of Contents

Introduction

I have watched the developments involving the native populations of Canada during my lifetime and am amazed by the one-sided opinions held by the powers-that-be in our nation. Knowledgeable people in decision-making positions have convinced themselves that they must look only at one side of this terrible situation and that rational thoughts, not politically correct and positive, from the native point of view must be eliminated or laundered to avoid offending someone. Any program with such an illogical base is doomed to failure, regardless of the subject.

I wish to start with an apology to all those who will, no doubt, be offended by my direct approach to these concerns. I do, however, hope that some of these thinkers and doers will not take the easy way out and simply dismiss me as a radical or a redneck, and that they will read my comments and give some soul-searching thought to my line of reasoning. My direct approach has developed over a lifetime of watching the wrong and ineffectual practices that have become the norm in dealing with the difficult situations faced by the natives of this country.

I do not pretend to be correct in every point I raise, though most of our policymakers and educators seem to feel they are. I am prepared to discuss any of my points of concern far more freely than many who perpetrate their marginalizing programs on the natives and on the entire population of Canada. Their false impressions of the native situation are presented to today's youth, and their young minds are being programmed by their school lessons. Our education system requires that students accept what is presented to them in the classroom; therefore, a great deal of correction is urgently needed in this area.

This writing is not intended to be an attack on all things native in Canada, but to point out some of the obvious facts that do not support the notion that all things native have always been wonderful and good. There are multiple facets to every bit of human history. By looking only at one facet, we cannot hope to gain even a partial understanding of the entirety. Our policymakers, politicians, educators, law enforcement officers, and other officials all seem to have themselves convinced that their one-sided position on these matters will help the natives. My long observations have lead me to believe that many of these programs will only ensure that the deplorable situations and the marginal existence that most native people have endured over the past 300 years or more will continue in perpetuity.

Please bear with me. I raise valid questions in these pages, questions that should be addressed by something more effective than pretense and embellishment. These common practices in the daily, ineffective dealings with natives do more damage than good, yet they are well guarded and insisted upon by the decision-makers and policy people of today.

Chapter 1
Aboriginal Situations in Canada

There are a variety of mindsets among the modern citizens of Canada about the situations faced by Canadian natives. This book is intended to be of some assistance to native people, many of whom, from my hands-on experienced viewpoint, appear to be in a fixed and non-productive mindset about their existence in the world.

My thoughts come about from frequent close contact with natives and from observations made over many years of police work among Canadian natives. The incidents and activities described in these pages may immediately be labeled as racist and hate literature by the Canadian powers-that-be because that is the quickest and easiest way to deal with the tragic situations the Canadian native people find themselves in, and have been in for the past 300 or more years. The long-established mindset among much of our current population and among the natives is damaging to the overall well-being of these people. Some action must be taken by the natives to demonstrate to us all where this harsh mindset is not accurate and to show that they are able and willing to demonstrate corrective action wherever these images are true.

I do not expect this book will produce good feelings in the people who take the time to read it. Most of this writing is based on a lifetime of work among and observation of the activities of aboriginal people, mainly in Alberta and British

Columbia. I have observed those in a position to deal with the native problems during those years as well, and it is difficult to be sure which side of this equation is more out of touch with reality. My observations, and those by others who have lived a parallel existence with me, are not put forth as being the exact model of every native person and native community in Canada. They are, however, the conclusions that many of us have come to over our years of first-hand observations of the Canadian natives in their day-to-day conduct.

There is a particularly evident aspect in these observations. Any of the native people who have chosen to take an active part in the world they were born into have quickly melded into the general, mixed population of Canada. Those who have chosen to remain on the reserves are the ones who are obvious to everyone who takes an interest in the native situation.

There is no doubt that some of the conclusions in the minds of these observers will leave some native persons with a genuine feeling of indignation. However, the primary purpose of this book is to point out the mindset that has developed among those of us who have been exposed directly to the conduct and behaviour of the natives over a long period of time and, to some extent, to show how and why these mindsets have developed.

There is no question that there are totally different thoughts and conclusions among many non-native Canadians today. I am of the opinion that most people from outside the native population, with their refined opinions, have gained their experience through reading, talking, schooling, and wishful thinking. Perhaps some have experienced a quick visit to some native settlements and, through the extensive application of sympathy and rose-coloured glasses, they have come to their erroneous conclusions.

The harsh observations and conclusions outlined here may not be totally correct in every instance; however, the majority are close to the true picture, as demonstrated by the natives during the time of their exposure to the new inhabitants. This writing is intended to show not only the mindsets that have been formed but also what contributed to these hard observations. These observations, in almost every situation, will also show the unwillingness and perhaps the inability of the Canadian aboriginals to become a part of the world into which they have been born.

Canadian natives have lived for many generations completely separated from their former ways of life. Many have contributed almost nothing to their daily human needs over those years, yet they make demands on others to fulfill their essential requirements. The world of today is perhaps not to their liking; however, this is the world as it exists, and their wishing for and demand for the return of impossible and bygone things will not bring about any real benefit for anyone. The deliberate and carefully planned alteration of the facts about the lives lived by the natives, both now and in the past, only adds to the difficulties for these people. By facing the realities, including those that are not complimentary of and ingratiating to the natives, we hope to make some progress with this major problem. Political correctness will have to be pushed aside to accomplish such an overdue appointment with reality.

Today, our modern country is faced with the all but impossible treaty agreements that were written hundreds of years ago. These treaties were prepared by people who had no idea how the country would change. The desires and needs of both the new settlers and the natives were different then from now. The people taking an active part in the country today, along with the majority of the natives, have different thought patterns.

Native demands for the settlement of treaties from hundreds of years ago become more impossible to meet with the passage of each year. The native people appear, in most cases, to feel they should be granted impossibly large tracts of land to enable them to return to their original ways of life. In other situations, the natives seem to feel that impossibly large cash payments would make their situation completely suitable. In reality, neither of these all-but-impossible solutions would have long-term benefits for either side. Today, we are all saddled with long-overdue settlements of the many treaties that have been outstanding for several hundred years, and the current mindsets leave all the aces in the hands of the natives.

The nation is left with the difficult task of trying to bring the native mindset into the realm of modern reality and to bring this about with the full understanding and cooperation of these people. The people who negotiated most of the treaties with the natives could not possibly have foreseen the situation we face today. These early citizens could not have imagined that the majority of the aboriginals would remain in the marginalizing lifestyles that the reserves and treaties prepared for them. The natives who have made the difficult choice to leave the reserves and become part of the new society have clearly demonstrated, in almost every case, that there is a productive and worthwhile life available to them, if they can only make this difficult move.

A recent book by Mr. Thomas King, *The Inconvenient Indian*, was released on August 13, 2013. The book contains arguments in favour of the natives of America being allowed to return to their allegedly ideal way of life, yet there are few concrete plans outlined that would make such an existence even remotely possible for these people. The original way of life of the natives in the pre-white invasion form would require the entire continent. These people may well be entitled to this dream existence in a more ideal world. However, this will not happen in the world that exists today. We do not need another royal commission of inquiry at great expense to come to the conclusion that this situation will not happen, even though there are valid arguments to support the claims by the natives. Such a just and proper situation could only have happened if the first explorers and discoverers had observed that the Americas were already inhabited by humanity and had simply sailed away to explore somewhere else.

Mr. King is obviously well educated and well read about the lives and struggles of nearly every native tribe in the world. He has attended the evil white man's universities; he has travelled extensively around the globe on modern aircraft; he has lived parts of his interesting life in a variety of locations throughout Canada and the United States. My conclusion from reading his account of his interesting life is that, while he is of native ancestry, he has completely adopted the ways and means of the invaders. His carefully thought-out positions in regard to the plight of the natives indicate a great deal of analysis on his part. His writing strongly supports the impossible position of the modern natives. However, he has not made more than some vague attempts to live that existence for himself and his family.

Most natives of today carry a deep-rooted feeling that they are being discriminated against by the Canadian majority. This feeling, no doubt, has some validity in some situations. I am in agreement in many ways with the person who said, "Racism most often has far more to do with conduct than with skin colour." The majority of the stories and examples in this book come from first-hand observations of the overall conduct of Canadian aboriginals in their daily activities, or non-activities, and will hopefully show some of the reasons behind these harsh conclusions by so many modern Canadians. The story is intended to provide some insight as to why and how the negative attitude among many Canadians came to be. Hopefully, they can be of assistance to all of us by demonstrating a gradual correction to the causes of the hard observations by so many of their fellow citizens.

Currently, and tragically, the conduct and attitude of many modern-day natives only adds to the harsh conclusions set out here. An obvious example is the aged native chief who recently appeared on national television in full feathered headdress and costume to flatly refuse to account for money made available to his tribe by our generous (in native funding) federal government. His costume was an obvious attempt to show native pride among his people and their history. However, it appears that he lost track of why he was being questioned. If he were to give just a moment of thought to the deplorable financial conduct by many native tribes across the nation in their handling of federally provided funds, he may find it somewhat difficult to pursue his present position of refusing to account for this money.

These are modern times. The funds made available to him and his tribe are from the assets of the long-established Canadian government and from the Canadian taxpaying citizens, yet this man does not feel he should be asked to account for any of this money. The days of wampum are gone; these payments are not for the purpose of convincing this man to sign some treaty agreement or to trick him out of his rightful territory. This money is to be used for food and shelter and the everyday needs of his people. This man should be asked to try to understand that the alleged evil done to the Canadian natives was perpetrated several hundred years ago and it is now too late to punish the persons responsible for those events, even if punishment in any form was a valid and required action.

A large portion of the native population in Canada has contributed little or nothing toward their own needs and desires over the past several hundred years, yet they feel justified in demanding more and better for themselves. Even if we were to give this chief the full benefit of the doubt and assume that he is one of the few who do not have a financial history he should not be proud of, he should not need to present such an image of outrage at being requested to account for these funds. With thoughts in mind of the current financial track records of many Canadian Indian bands, many of us will be amazed if this man does not have some compelling reasons of his own to fight this new government request for accounting by his tribe and himself.

This man may well be among the many native leaders who draw higher salaries than our prime minister or the provincial premiers, and this could be only the tip of the iceberg. Given the history in Canada in regard to financial mismanagement by a large number of the native tribes, he should be able to understand why our leaders ask for better accounting by him and his people. The current attitude of sympathy for the natives among a large number of modern Canadian citizens serves as fuel for men like this chief. He can hardly be faulted for riding this gift horse as far and as hard as he is allowed to. The old saying of "never get off a winning horse" most certainly could apply here.

Chapter 2
Native Heroes

There have been truly great people from among the Canadian natives over the last few centuries and some of them were not dealt with in the way they should have been. This conduct is another tragedy in our history; however, some aspects of this mistreatment came about, to some extent, from unacceptable behaviour by the majority of their fellow natives. Native men have served with distinction in the Canadian military in both World Wars and in the other conflicts of recent history. They were reported to have been exceptional in their service as snipers in the First World War. A number have received military honors for outstanding conduct in action. Many native soldiers became well known for their steadfastness and obvious bravery under the life-and-death conditions of a battlefield.

These great citizens chose to serve their country and they did so with distinction. Some of these native returning soldiers have, perhaps, not been dealt with by their country as they should have been. However, this lack of appreciation was definitely not only for native soldiers, but for many of our distinguished citizens on their return from war. This aspect of our history is definitely not one to bring about feelings of pride and accomplishment, and there are many other examples. We do not need to develop and embellish other aspects of our history that induce national feelings of discomfort and shame. History is exactly that; it cannot be changed.

Chapter 3
Before Written History

In prehistoric times, the natives of the Americas were spread from the southern tip of South America to the farthest northern point of the high Arctic. These people were tough and determined beyond what we consider to be tough and hardy today. Many of the people who lived in the far north had no knowledge of conditions anywhere else on the globe or on this continent. They were obviously not living there by choice. In spite of this, they still must be considered for their determination and wealth of survival skills. They lived in climactic conditions that could be described as near impossible to survive in even with access to the skills and equipment of modern man.

The natives of Central and South America and the southern portion of North America developed complicated societal structures in the thousand years beginning roughly around 1000 BC. Sadly, the most well known of these populations collapsed long before the arrival of the first foreigners for reasons that present-day people can only speculate about. Detailed studies of these lost civilizations indicates that their collapse may have been due to a variety of situations, ranging from tribal warfare to the overuse of the available lands so that crop failure brought about mass starvation. The possibility of prehistoric climate change may also have been a factor in their demise.

The original spread of humanity across the land is a subject that can only be speculated about. Today, we could easily believe that the Innu and Eskimo people had been forced to take up residence on that portion of the land. This theory applies well if we assume that the climate conditions in those areas were the same then as they are now. The presence of those peoples in that part of the landmass leaves us to speculate that they were either forced by stronger tribes and warfare or that the north had a much warmer climate at the time of their arrival and they learned to survive over the centuries upon the gradual development of the present arctic climatic conditions.

A careful review of the climatic conditions that exist today over the entire landmass, and in Canada in particular, will raise more questions than answers. Assuming that the natives of the northern interior regions of British Columbia and the Canadian prairies originated in the coastal areas, then the same questions come into play in those territories. The possibility of a much more hospitable climate at the time of their arrival must be considered as a valid point, more than them having been forced into these harsh living areas by tribal warfare. War would have pushed these people into these harsh climates in a sudden way, creating a situation that would not have allowed them time to learn necessary survival skills. Climate change over several centuries would have provided that opportunity for them. Hard evidence from around the world seems to back the convictions of many of us that survival is possible under the extreme conditions of the Arctic, yet man cannot survive in the opposite conditions of high heat and lack of water without an abundance of outside aid.

Chapter 4
Right of Possession

The native populations of North America were totally taken by surprise by the first arrivals of foreigners on this continent. The natives were thinly distributed over the entire continent, having found an existence in even the most unwelcoming areas, such as the high Arctic. The natives that the newcomers first encountered had found an easier living among the abundant natural food sources of the coastal areas and along the rivers leading inland from the more hospitable coasts. Most of the natives were non-aggressive toward the newcomers and they seemed to be fascinated by their ways and methods. It seems obvious from the complete lack of questions or restriction of access that there was little or no thought among these people about who was rightfully in possession of the land or territories.

There was evidence of distrust and hatred among the many tribal groups whom the new people encountered. Early records indicate there was primitive warfare between most tribes or regional groups. Prisoners were often taken during these primitive wars and these unfortunate people became slaves to the members of the victorious tribes. The overtaken territories were occupied by the stronger tribe until some more powerful war party took it away from them, perhaps after a century or more.

Today, dedicated students of native non-history pretend that the natives of North America had as complicated a land title system as that developed by centuries of disciplined learning in many other areas of our Earth. A look at the limited history of pre-invasion North America should raise more questions than answers in this regard.

Contrary to the teachings of leaders and scholars of today, the lives and lifestyles of the original natives were not the perfect existence promoted among us today. False information about the native existence is promoted among us today because of the need in our modern world to be politically correct, non-offensive, and proper. Life was a continuous struggle for these people, yet they seemed to be content with their lot and they made little or no effort to improve their difficult situation. Perhaps religion or superstitious beliefs brought them to accept their way of life as though it was the will of some greater being. Their chosen existence left them where, if they were not under attack from a neighbouring tribe, they were experiencing hunger or bone-chilling exposure, or any other of the trials and tests that come from being in complete harmony and surrender to the continual cycles of nature.

The native people of those times lived with the ebb and flow of nature and, to their credit, they found a coexistence with nature that they seemed willing to accept and endure. The word *endure* is used because that condition is common among creatures, including humanity, who choose to live within the constant fluctuations that are a dominant feature of nature.

Unfortunately, there are no records or actual history available about the natives of most of the Americas or we might be more able to ascertain the actual time that this part of the world has been occupied by these people. There are strong indications that humanity has been present in the Americas for perhaps as long as on any other part of the globe. This strong possibility leads to valid questions about the accepted existence among the natives of North America.

However, this narrative is more directed toward those in that territory that was to become Canada.

The time of arrival of humanity in the Americas is debatable; however, there is no doubt that it will be measured in many thousands of years rather than hundreds. Perhaps millions of years would be an appropriate measure when we consider the strong possibility that the Arctic regions must have experienced more hospitable climatic conditions at the time the Inuit and Eskimos settled there. With such an amount of time involved, many more questions arise. Obviously, the natives of this part of the world were content with whatever nature provided or they would have struggled for change and improved stability in their lives. To their credit, these people accepted life as it happened; perhaps superstition or religious beliefs or simply the lack of drive and ambition led to their reluctance to experiment with new methods that might have produced a more stable living for some or all of them.

The new arrivals from the Old World were from a lifestyle that required them to fight nature on many fronts in their continuous efforts to prevent winter starvation or death by freezing or exposure. These people worked throughout their lives in their self-imposed struggles to improve and protect their lives and those of their loved ones. The new people were constantly improving their quality of life and bettering their living standards. Life had much greater value in the minds of the new arrivals and they must have been quite baffled by the almost total lack of such concerns among the natives. The newcomers had long ago taught themselves to read and write and they had, for centuries, recorded every success and failure they encountered in their efforts to live and to improve their methods of creating a reliable lifestyle. The new arrivals were, no doubt, shocked to observe the laid-back attitude and methods practiced among the North American natives. These new people could clearly see that the lives and the longevity of the natives were left to the fickle whims of nature.

In spite of these facts, the modern descendants of the original people of North America, along with the descendants of many of the original traders and settlers, developed a mindset that places the entire fault for the current native situation on the hands and minds of the original new arrivals and all their descendants. This mindset may seem to be quite valid in the imagination established in our modern world. However, there are valid arguments that suggest the natives themselves must also accept a large portion of the fault or blame surrounding their current situations.

Finding of fault or blame will not go far toward solving the terrible situations among the natives of today. The fact remains that equal distribution of fault or negligence with the modern-day natives would establish a more balanced view and assessment and, hopefully, a willingness to work toward making changes among themselves that could improve their current circumstances.

The present viewpoint propagated by the natives and a large majority of today's non-native Canadian citizens only brings a continuation of the deplorable situations that can be observed on almost every native reserve community in this country. The longer this one-way blame continues, with a void of responsibility on the other side, the longer the self-defeating mindset of the natives will thrive.

More than 300 years have passed with little or no change in the native attitude. However, with the continuation of the present mindset and actions, we can be sure that the past few hundred years have only been the beginning of this deplorable situation. Change and improvement for the natives can only come about if they are placed in or if they get themselves into a mindset where they feel some responsibility for their everyday needs and requirements. Such a mindset would bring about efforts on their part to change their thinking and actions along this line and in parallel with those who support our modern nation with a generous portion of our incomes. There is no doubt that history holds some hard and ugly facts in the background of every one of the tribes and nationalities of humanity, but there are none of us who can truthfully say "The world owes me a living," just because of some happening in history.

Chapter 5
Finding Fault

The leaders of the ancestors of our present-day natives should not be judged to be totally without responsibility in the establishment of the current native situation in Canada. Those people, and most certainly the leaders at the time of discovery, had an obligation to protect and preserve their allegedly cherished way of life. Their responsibility was the same as that of every other segment of humanity since the beginnings of human history, anywhere on the globe.

The undeniable and continuous intertribal warfare should tell us what these early leaders had to be prepared for and constantly aware of. They needed to be continuously ready for quick changes in their plans and actions to ensure the safety and security of their people. They had to keep their followers constantly prepared to fend off or to attack the neighbouring tribe. If they failed in this responsibility, they would be vanquished and become slaves to the victorious tribe.

The present-day natives are convinced that the causes of their current situation are entirely the responsibility of the new arrivals, and they are encouraged in this belief by their modern-day leaders, a large percentage of our present population, and most of our modern politicians. The main themes of modern education vilify every action by our leaders and decision-makers in the early times of Canadian colonization. The leaders of our governments of those times of harsh reality were certainly not as sympathetic to the natives as our majority is today. However, we can be quite sure they were not as vicious and cruel as modern school lessons indicate.

Our students are taught that the original traders and settlers had no respect for the rights of the natives and, in fact, they are portrayed as wanting the native people "out of their way." If modern lessons were accurate and the original decision-makers had been only partially as cruel and uncaring as they are alleged to have been, the native situation would be different today. The earliest Canadian governments had a system similar to that of today's. This new government was patterned after the governments of the new citizens from a variety of places in the Old World. There would have been an opposition group who would have been outspoken about every action by the government, including the treatment of and plans for the native situations.

The faults involved in the colonization of this country must be distributed to both factions of the population. The earliest arrivals from the Old World were traders and explorers. These men were drawn by ambition and curiosity and found themselves in the New World for long periods of time, or for all their lives in many cases. The need of humanity for companionship and sex was as strong among these men as it has been in humans since the beginning of time. These men found that their natural urges were stronger than their upbringing and they abandoned many of their religious and moral lessons from their earlier years in their homelands.

There are stories in the history of those early years of men who bragged of having more than a dozen native wives. These temporary unions contributed to the establishment and abundance of the Metis people who, in a short time, were so numerous that there was thought of declaring them as another tribe or nationality in this country. This conduct by these men is certainly nothing short of despicable, but the facts are there in abundance and nothing will change the impact of their actions.

If we look at the other side, we raise valid questions for the native side of these equations. It can be readily seen that intertribal breeding among the natives was prevented by the hate and distrust generated by their primitive territorial wars. The sudden arrival of the new people brought another aspect to the fore among the native people; suddenly, they were faced with new people living among them and they were unprepared for the almost natural consequences. There is an abundance of evidence of an almost total lack of moral conduct among the natives in this regard. Perhaps the native respect for nature in all its variety did not bring about jealousy and envy among the native males. The non-actions by the native men of those times is difficult to contemplate if we are to look from our modern thought patterns and conduct of today. Obviously, they applied a different standard to their family making and moral conduct than our modern societies.

The children of these casual encounters were left with their native families and raised along with their full-blooded relatives. The separation between the native tribes and the half-breed offspring is something of a mystery. There seems to have been some action among the natives to push these impure offspring away from their families, forcing them to establish tribes or clans of their own. Obviously, this action among the tribes was not all-encompassing, as many of these people of mixed blood remained with their maternal families.

Today, there are few people among the natives who can claim to be full-blood natives. This dilution of native blood produced a different appearance among many of these people than was the standard at the time of the arrival of the first foreigners. There are people today who identify themselves as native yet have green or blue eyes and hair colour far lighter than that of the original natives.

Modern-day politicians are so afraid of losing votes that they will say and do strange things to appease the natives. This situation brings the current Canadian taxpaying citizens to face the fact that a large block of votes will go to whichever politician is the most accommodating and obliging to the natives. This brings a related topic to the foreground: the fact that the modern-day natives in Canada have a vote but are almost totally tax-exempt. Most of us in the modern world should, with only a minimum of analytical thought, see this as a totally unworkable situation. There was obviously some hope and thought about bringing the natives into the New World and the new lifestyle by granting them the vote. This move was no doubt planned and taken as a method of instilling some interest in our system of government and to bring the majority of Canadian natives into a new status as fully understanding and responsible citizens.

I am certainly not suggesting that present-day natives should lose their vote. I am of the opinion that there should be educational programs among them to cause a better understanding of this important aspect of a democracy. The original plan was to bring about awareness among the natives and, perhaps, even some respect, so they would see the positive aspects of taking part in the new society and its unfamiliar methods of government. This goal has not been attained in the all-encompassing way that is needed. The native lack of understanding and disinterest is still there, in spite of incentives and financial benefits and encouragements.

The natives of today are mainly heard from when they are opposing a new development by some branch or corporation of the dominant Canadian society. There have been few recent developments by our industries that have not encountered vigorous opposition from the natives in some or all of their locations. There is little doubt that large "under the table" payments have been forthcoming from industries that found they must establish some new project to preserve their share of world market and their competitive advantages in both local and world trade. These payments or bribes will have gone to the native leaders who then told their loyal subjects that the new move by the evil whites could be given their approval.

The natives have no regard for the needs of trade and commerce because their past experiences have shown them that there will always be another area for them to attack. They have also learned that the success or failure of any program or development by the whites will have no long-term effect on their lives. Native leaders have learned that if they play their cards correctly they will benefit in a financial way, depending on how vigorously they oppose whatever development is attempted. The present financial histories among the many native tribes are another clear indication of "under the table" payments from corporations and perhaps even government programs where the action was important to our progress as a nation.

The presence of corruption in so many of the tribal leaders certainly comes into play for such an action by whoever is charged with the responsibility of obtaining the necessary clearances. Many among us today are encouraged to believe that these protests are due to the inherent native concern for the environment and wellbeing of the creatures of nature. This may be the situation with some people, but there have been many situations where other motivations are evident—the leading motivational force being money, in huge amounts, but only for the benefit of the leaders.

Chapter 6
Greed and Incompetence

Many of the native leaders in modern Canada, along with many other citizens, desire to have large amounts of money at their disposal. There is little room for doubt that many of us would be caught up in the same greed and misappropriation if we were granted access to the huge amounts of money that are made available to the natives on a regular and unchecked basis. The temptation would increase if we could be fairly certain no punitive action would result upon being questioned or caught in the act. Many of the natives who have, by politics or other means, become part of the management of the various tribes have clearly demonstrated their greed in instances where they have access to an opportunity to help themselves to funds provided to assist the majority of their people. Often, there seems to be no bounds to the greed displayed.

There are, without doubt, some instances where people have had access to such opportunities but avoided the temptation to help themselves and have instead seen to the proper and intended use of these large amounts of government money. The tragic fact is that such incidents are rare; perhaps our government should establish a reward program for any native or group of natives who clearly identify an instance where funds were put to the proper and intended use.

Among the greatest tragedies is the continuous pouring out of money to native tribes across the country with no thought to the obvious abuse and misuse of it. The massive federal government Department of Aboriginal Affairs and Northern Development should be held to the fire for their continuous supplying of our money to this nationwide sinkhole. All these government people must be blind and deaf and unable to think, or they just don't care.

The tragic events at Attawapiskat in relatively recent times are a clear demonstration of this weakness among many of these people. The tragic choice by our decision-makers to not deal with criminal actions at Attawapiskat and similar situations can only be viewed as an invitation for others to do likewise. Our expensive Supreme Court (locally known as "the bureau of criminal rights") has paved the way for the continued abuse of government funds by their continual failures to deal with criminal actions among the natives. This elevated group of highly educated Canadians is obviously unable to see the long-term effects of their gutless position of non-enforcement.

The material in the following paragraphs is based on information researched and prepared by the Canadian Taxpayers Association; only a few items have been quoted here to demonstrate the point in this chapter. The original documents from the Taxpayers Association include the highest salaries drawn by 200 of the chiefs and executive members of native tribes across Canada, along with many other facts. The numbers were obtained from a recent federal government program that requires the chief and counsel of all Indian bands to disclose their income from their position in the tribe. Some tribal leaders have complied with this law but there are still many more who have not.

There is a situation for many of the natives across Canada with this government action in that their tribal beliefs and cultures have placed their chosen leaders in exalted positions where they shall not be questioned by anyone under any circumstances. These folks are considered near-sacred and are protected in the native culture. The most flagrant demonstrations of this widespread greed seem to be perpetrated by British Columbia and Alberta tribal leaders and their councils.

The chief of the Kwikwetlem band—this is most likely the Coquitlam, British Columbia, band—of eighty-two members drew a total income last year of $914,219 from his position as chief. This breaks down to an annual cost of $11,149 for each of his eighty-two band members. The Shuswap band of eighty-seven members shows the combined salary of their chief and only one of the councilors at $404,413. This partial number amounts to an annual cost of $4,648 for each of the reserve residents. The native band at Fort McKay, Alberta, has 395 members. The chief and council there draw a total income of $1,708,097, which breaks down to a cost of $4,324 for each resident of the reserve.

There are many such examples in the numbers provided by the Taxpayers Association; however, these do seem to be the worst of them. The figures used for these examples do not include expenses or benefits claimed by these chiefs and councilors. We must search our own minds to determine what each of us would do in a circumstance where we were given access to huge amounts of money every year and could easily help ourselves to a generous portion of it. The decision would be made even more difficult to resist if we could be quite sure that there would be no criminal charges or demands to repay the money even in the off-chance that we were caught. Another addition to the native leaders' temptations is that most of their own local citizens do not seem to resent their unabashed greed.

I hope never to face such a temptation. The fact that these salaries or wages or fraudulently obtained monies are totally tax-free must be borne in mind as this information is processed through our thoughts.

Recent research of the Internet shows that every Canadian native is also receiving an annual sum to reimburse them for the tax that is paid at the till for their individual purchases of tobacco and fuel.

The mayor of Toronto, with a population of over five million, draws a salary of $177,499, which breaks down to a cost of approximately one-third of one cent for each resident. The mayor of Vancouver, with a population of over two million, draws an annual salary of $155,612, which breaks down to a cost of seven one-hundredths of one cent for each citizen. The expenses and benefits for these two mayors are not included here and could make some difference in these figures. These salaries are entirely taxable.

The annual salaries of the mayors of ten smaller cities across Canada were obtained and examined to determine the cost per citizen. These annual costs ranged from a low of thirty-eight one-hundredths of one cent to a high of $2.06. The average for these ten was $1.12 for each citizen.

31

Chapter 7
Common Political Interests

Our politicians and the leaders in the native communities of today have a significant common interest in their combined desire to stop any proposed legislation that would make them more accountable for their often-exorbitant salaries and their astonishing expense accounts. With this common interest shared between the native leaders and many of our elected representatives, they are able to work out deals between them that are truly disgusting. The earlier reference to the native chief appearing in full feathered costume to protest the government request for some accounting of the money granted to him and his tribe will again arise in this dialogue. This man is definitely "on the same page" as many of our recent politicians, in regard to those who wish to know what has become of the taxpayers' money.

These nosey people must be convinced that the pay and allowances of our native leaders are something that should not be questioned under any circumstance. The ideal situation in the minds of these people would be patterned after the methods and accepted circumstances that have been in place among most native tribes for eons. The native leaders have been looked upon as near-sacred in their culture; this may be a large part of the inability among victimized tribes to mount resistance or to call for accounting from their fraudulent leaders.

Many of today's politicians look only from their modern-day viewpoint, which is geared to the question,

"What would we do today if we came upon a new landmass on this planet and there were people already there?" This mindset is wonderfully benevolent and easily adopted because most of us are certain that no such place exists. What we would do and how we would conduct ourselves in this imaginary situation is an easy scenario to address. It becomes immediately complicated if we allow ourselves to look back to our forefathers and their mindsets and motivations when the first of them began to arrive in the New World. These people came from a different set of circumstances and a different background than the natives of those times. We should stop overlooking these facts when we make scholarly efforts at soul searching and fault finding from our comfortable Western world of today. We owe a debt of gratitude to those early settlers and explorers; however, in our modern times, we find only the motivation to damn them at every opportunity in our false hope of appeasing another section of humanity.

The modern-day natives have found a "cash cow" and they cannot be faulted for taking full advantage of it. The rewards to the natives for such conduct in recent history are abundant and they continue in spite of the tragic records of corruption, fraud, and favouritism around nearly every such cash grant in our history.

Chapter 8
Verbal History

The natives and their leaders frequently talk of their wonderful historical knowledge and how they passed it verbally from one generation to the next. These people claim an ability with oral history that exceeds any similar method among all of humanity anywhere on our globe. Many modern thinkers and doers are fully prepared to make decisions and give their approval on vague rumors based on native oral history. Many of these modern thinkers will vigorously promote the vague possibility of native oral history being even vaguely near to the actual facts.

Many of us will remember the classroom game we learned in public school where a simple phrase was whispered to the first student in a line and then it was whispered from one to the next until it reached the last of the line. We were all amazed at the total lack of similarity between the beginning phrase and the ending one. My grade school teacher took this game one short step further by giving the first student a written message, which was passed down the line to clearly demonstrate the effectiveness of the written word.

Now we are asked to believe and take lessons from rumors about native histories that were entirely verbal. About forty-five years ago, a native man wrote a letter to the editor of the *Williams Lake Tribune* newspaper during a heated situation involving racial conflict. He expressed an accurate description of oral history in his letter. The following is a direct quote from his letter, although he was directing his comments only toward the inability of the non-native Canadians to pass information verbally.

I suppose that anybody with brains like a human ought to know that rumor, going from one mouth to another, can add from two sentences to double that when it comes out of the second person's mouth.

This man would have to play a different word game if he was now to write about the oral legends passed by the natives over the centuries of their non-written history. Today, the Canadian natives and many well-educated Canadians from the entire population believe in and ask us all to believe in the accuracy and reliability of native oral history.

This unquestionable belief applies only if the information was perpetrated by natives and it carries a positive message, as all their chosen history does. Some thought should be directed to the oral history of any of the many native intertribal wars. Some of these wars went on sporadically over many years, with neither side becoming a genuine victor. The oral history of Tribe A will certainly be quite opposite to that of Tribe B. Should any of our modern scholars be prepared to deny this very human circumstance, then I would suggest they should give their head a good shaking.

Chapter 9
Accepting Some Fault

A positive aspect of accepting even a small portion of the fault for the current situation among the natives of today would provide them with a goal to work toward. If they were to say that portion X of the situation is of their own doing and if there is fault attached it is theirs and theirs alone, these people might be more willing and able to make some changes in their own conduct to deal with that particular aspect of their modern existence. All of us know that the things that affect us directly, and especially those of our own doing, are things that can and must be dealt with by ourselves. We can request or demand that others correct these things; however, the result of these corrections, if any, will be marginal or less. There is great wisdom in the old saying "If you want something done properly, do it yourself." This is a wonderful concept but it does involve that ugly four-letter word, *work*.

The news media today is full of stories about the plight of our natives, but there is an obvious lack of accountability or even the suggestion of some responsibility on the native side of this equation. There is no question that the natives have found themselves in a situation that most seem to be unable to cope with. The accepted methods of survival among the natives for thousands of years have left an attitude that is counter-productive in the world of today. The combined efforts of the natives and Canadian society to make the native situation better have been a dismal failure and our combined efforts today are prolonging this tragedy.

Natives today demand they be granted huge tracts of land for their exclusive use and self-determination. This approach is unrealistic. Few areas in this country are suitable for such an endeavor, and even in the few locations where land is available, as in Alaska, the agreements are elusive. A tentative agreement was reached in the Alaska situation in 1972 but has not been finalized in the forty-three years since. There is no doubt that a portion of the delay is deliberate, brought about by the state and federal officials, but there are also aspects of the non-agreement from the native side of the equation.

In the Alaska situation, many of the natives involved are not satisfied with the requirement that they relinquish their hunting and fishing rights to other parts of the state. The combined non-agreement skills have left this massive agreement in limbo for more than two generations.

If such an agreement were to be reached in Canada, we would all be expected to believe that the natives would truly use self-determination and be completely independent. With the records of the past 300 or more years, there should be many questions about how this giant step could be possible. The current attitude among many modern Canadians would require our immediate assistance to these independent natives before the first winter had established itself. If we give any thought to the track records of gross mismanagement among the majority of the modern-day natives, it is abundantly obvious that these people could not suddenly find the drive and resources among themselves to manage such a vast undertaking. Obviously, they would resent any controls or governance of such an endeavor and would, without doubt, be once again in a situation where they are cold and starving.

Charles Scheideman

News reports about native situations tell us that an extremely high percentage of Canadian prison inmates are of aboriginal origin. Missing and murdered women are almost entirely natives. The number of children taken into government care facilities due to family neglect is also largely made up of natives. A number not commonly quoted by news gatherers is the high percentage of natives among the many children born in Canada with fetal alcohol syndrome. Research into the ancestral history of alcohol abusers among our modern society would be politically incorrect and therefore must be left undone or unreported.

All these tragedies are lumped together and blamed on the descendants of the first new citizens to arrive here. Blame has no beneficial effect for anyone, but the continual pretending that blame lies with only one side of this tragedy is far more damaging to everyone involved than the factual analysis of the entire situation. The effects of this one-sided situation are obvious to those among us who have taken some interest in the eventual correction of this impossible thing.

A frank examination of the entire native situation would produce a much better understanding and acknowledgement of the sad realities of it and would provide some basis for the eventual correction of some of these awful situations. Such a direct and pointed examination would force the native population and the current Canadian bureaucrats and do-gooders to have a realistic look at the entire matter with less finger pointing and blind acceptance of fault.

One of these obvious but ugly facts is that if any identifiable group of women among our modern society were to conduct themselves in the same way that many native women do, and have done for a long time, this new group might immediately displace native women as the most murdered and missing people in Canada. This is truly awful, yet our politicians and even some of our police leaders are crying out for another detailed and expensive inquiry into why so many of these murdered and missing people are natives.

If any of these misguided, inquiring people had ever been near a predominantly native community in this country for more than a brief visit and allowed themselves to observe the conduct of many of these people, they could not possibly see, or try to justify, the need for another detailed and expensive investigation. If our present decision-makers decide upon another detailed examination, an obvious problem will again rise to the surface. The causes of this situation are already firmly established in the minds of these inquiring people. The inquiry will involve the preparation of a detailed list of actions by our dominant society that caused this tragedy among the natives. The truth and many of the ugly facts will be overlooked.

If we must go through another useless and expensive inquiry into these issues, it should be broadened to look at all killings and missing persons wherever a native person is involved. The inquiry or examination should look at all native murders, including males, native on native, other race on native, and native on another race.

The routine conduct of these people is the primary cause of their leading position in these gruesome statistics and this awful fact must be dealt with by the natives themselves with some reasonable assistance from the huge bureaucracy that has arisen around the native situation in Canada. The criminals and perverts who prey on people who conduct themselves in that way will always be among us. Perhaps our dominant society will someday learn how to lessen this ugly fact, but until that day comes, vitally necessary and corrective changes must be made by the

Charles Scheideman

natives, with some assistance from the huge native-assisting bureaucracy. Another sad fact that is seldom made an issue is that about 70 percent of the murdered native women were killed by other natives.

Chapter 10
Look From Both Sides

These thoughts are being put to paper with the hope that they will cause the reader to look from another possible and plausible viewpoint when they consider the tragic situation that our native population faces today. Our current mindset and that of the recent past has been distorted by our leaders and the native leaders who strive to place the entire fault on our Old World ancestors, these ancestors who fought an epic struggle with nature and the elements just to get here.

The native populations of Canada were well established, and had been for centuries, when the foreigners began to come on the scene, yet they chose to do little about an event that should have been obviously not to their common good. This ugly fact becomes even more evident if we accept the fabrications about the grand and glorious living conditions of our natives prior to the arrival of the invaders. These people would have been much more prepared to defend such a grand existence if it had been even partially factual. The few native populations who had recently occupied some taken-over tribal territory were not in as firm a position as many of their contemporary people to judge and react to the arrivals of the newcomers. However, this situation was not in the majority. If we give these early arrivals some thought, we must come to the conclusion that the natives of Canada should have known, or at least have had strong suspicions, that this major event was the beginning of the end of their allegedly cherished way of life.

Since the beginnings of human history, we have experienced the need to defend ourselves and our chosen way of life. Those who couldn't or didn't are gone, or they have been absorbed into a new society, with the exception of the Canadian natives. Over the course of history, people around the world who did not take a successful defensive position have been wiped out, with few survivors, if any, left to adapt to and accept the changed world. This tragic reality is due mainly to the territorial, aggressive, and generally mean-spirited nature of humanity, although many of the new arrivals to the Americas may have arrived with thoughts of actually improving the living conditions of the natives.

Contrary to the teaching of today, many areas clearly demonstrated where the Canadian natives, with some relatively simple changes, could have made their living conditions better with some help and guidance from the newcomers. Relatively minor changes to their living and survival methods could have brought, and in many cases did bring, better longevity and more comfortable living to the natives.

Human history from all over this world, as tragic as it is, has always shown that mankind had to be prepared to defend their way of life, what they had, and what they hoped to gain for themselves. Where their defense was not properly applied, or where it was inadequate, those people lost their cherished way of life. The natives of Canada are one of the few peoples to have an exception from this cruel and inconsiderate fact of life; however, they have failed to recognize their unique position.

Chapter 11
Primitive Wars

Our ancestors arrived in North America to find a human population at a stage of evolution that had not advanced to the point where they could work together for the good of their entire number. Although most will vigorously deny this fact, at the time of the first offshore arrivals, North American natives were fighting among themselves along almost every tribal boundary on the entire continent. This primitive fighting and taking of slaves may have eventually led to amalgamation of some tribes or the destruction of others, as occurred between the Iroquois and the Huron just as the first traders and settlers began to appear. There is little room for doubt that similar wipeouts occurred in many other areas of North America.

This is another fact that casts doubt on the alleged wonderful lifestyles of the natives of North America. There is no recorded history before the arrival of the traders and settlers and the much-touted oral history among the native people would certainly not have included such negative details. Human nature in its most primitive form anywhere on this globe would have attended to that possibility in a thorough way had they been relying on oral history. Humanity learned long ago to put aside unpleasant memories. The oral history passed between generations of the North American natives should not be given more than a brief acknowledgement. Recorded history and, therefore, valid knowledge clearly sets out this fact.

Natives of North America had no realization that there were other segments of humanity on this globe until some of our ancestors began to arrive on the shores. Today, we flog the memories of our ancestors and lay blame on them because they chose to settle in and make a life for themselves. They did not necessarily do this with a view to destroying or severely altering the native way of life but, possibly, with thoughts of making a better life for themselves and the natives. Our ancestors found people wherever they ventured in their early explorations. They saw living conditions and survival methods that were far more primitive than the systems the newcomers had chosen to leave in their homelands. No doubt some of these new arrivals saw an opportunity to simply take over a country; however, a large percentage of the new arrivals believed they could teach some of their methods to the natives and bring about a rapid improvement to the native way of existence. These vastly superior methods had been developed and, most importantly, recorded over centuries in the homeland of the new arrivals and could be easily demonstrated to the natives.

Many believed they could help the natives and that the natives could quickly improve their primitive and marginal existence. Many of these newcomers were willing and able to provide some help and direction to the natives to make necessary changes to what the settlers had observed to be inadequate and inefficient methods. Many of the changes would not have forced huge alterations to the native way of living; however, a large number of these changes would have brought positive results for the native people.

The newcomers to North America came from areas where the written word was no longer considered unique or new. They understood the advances that a written language had made available to them. Every aspect of their Old World existence had been improved by these reading and writing skills. The new people came from areas where humanity had long ago developed permanent methods of recording matters of importance. The written word was vital to the progress and advancements of their civilizations. Many of the new people had experience with the development of their written languages and most had the ability to read and write. Many of these new people had read material from the massive printing presses that quickly produced the written words so vital to their constant struggle to improve their lives.

The earliest attempts in the Old World at making records and written words began about 9,000 years before the first explorers arrived in the Americas. The knowledge and understanding that resulted from the written word was largely responsible for the events that brought explorers and settlers to every location on our globe. Without a written language, the knowledge required to accurately navigate the oceans of the world could not have developed.

Today, we, as Canadians, are told in a convincing manner that these developments by humanity around the globe have been nothing but evil and destructive to the Canadian native way of existence. A thorough examination of the original native ways, right up to modern times, clearly shows that these people have forever been willing to put all these new methods to use, if only for their own convenience. They do, however, dwell on the alleged negative effects of the new technology on almost every aspect of their old ways.

Chapter 12
Whiskey Trade

There is no doubt that, among the new arrivals to Canada, there were some with criminal tendencies who would bring their criminal skills to play if any opportunity was to present itself. Some immediately saw the native weakness, or perhaps it would be better described as their allergic reaction, to alcohol, and did not hesitate to take advantage of it.

The whiskey trade began to flourish, and in a few years had blossomed into a major problem. The whiskey trade was largely responsible for the formation of the North West Mounted Police in 1873 and was the primary reason for the establishment of the native residential schools around that same time.

We Canadians like to claim that the evil whiskey traders all came across the international boundary from the United States, but this is unlikely. A great deal of the whiskey came out of the United States as a legitimate trade product because the skills and equipment to manufacture this product, along with the agricultural activities to produce the required grain, were more advanced in the longer-established populations of the United States.

Today, we are told that the residential school system is largely responsible for the extensive alcohol abuse among the natives. It is of interest that the earliest schools were established in the last years of the decade of 1870–1880, yet the whiskey trade had flourished long enough before that time that the North West Mounted Police were established in 1873. This is a clear example of present-day scholars and politicians embellishing the facts to make their fabrications stronger. The residential schools were negative in many ways, but we can be sure they had nothing to do with the cause of the alcohol abuse and the negative attitude among the natives, then or now.

The natives in particular, but all of us today, are taught that fur traders and settlers arrived with nothing but aggression in their minds and on their agendas. Contrary to these teachings and beliefs, there is a good possibility that many of the new arrivals landed here believing they could and would make life better and more comfortable for the natives. There is no doubt that such a suggestion is contrary to the modern position taken by both the natives and the majority of present-day Canadians; however, it is presented here as food for thought.

It raises a valid question. Could this have been the mindset of many of our ancestors on their arrival here? There was certainly ample evidence available to these new arrivals to support such a conclusion. These new arrivals observed a lifestyle and living conditions among the natives far inferior to those the new people had chosen to leave behind in their former countries. The statistical data recorded since their arrival shows there are far more people here today who identify themselves as natives than when the first explorers landed. This fact clearly indicates that the native populations of Canada have a higher overall survival rate since the arrival of the foreigners, yet they continuously complain about their loss of culture and lifestyle.

There is little room to argue that the world might be in a healthier state today if all of humanity had lived by the rules of nature as the North American natives did during their pre-discovery time. Nature, without the diligent efforts of some of mankind, would probably have reduced or slowed the overpopulation we face today.

Today, there is an obvious change in the appearance of many of those who identify themselves as natives. Many of the natives who were the first to be met by the new explorers and settlers had a different appearance to those we see in modern times. This change in appearance is due not only to the different dress of today but also due to the ancestries and bloodlines of these people. The many years in close proximity with the newcomers brought about changes. The bloodlines of many natives have been diluted by their close proximity to the new people.

Many of the positive or negative effects of these changes are still to be assessed, but there seems to be little opportunity for optimism. Our historical records make frequent reference to the mixed-blood people all across the nation. The history of the Riel Rebellion is an obvious example of this fact. There are records of early thoughts among people from those times to actually declare the Metis or mixed blood people as another tribal group among all the others. There are indications that such actions were started in various places across the nation.

Chapter 13
Mindset of the New People

Rather than glorifying the imaginary way of life among the natives of those pre-explorer times, we should research the origins and background of the early pioneers. These people came from a long history of learning about and recording their life experiences and the skills that worked well for them and their ancestors. In spite of this, they chose to leave and start over in the new land. An examination of Old World ways is simple and accurate because of the written histories from those parts of the world.

What could have been in the history of these people that motivated them to gather the strength and ambition to travel halfway around the globe in pursuit of vague rumors about what may be there? These people were cut from tough material. They had an inner drive to work and succeed. They set out with questionable transportation to go somewhere they had little knowledge of, and they came forward in thousands. If we give some thought to these facts, we must come to the conclusion that life for these people could not have been all good in their homelands. Had life in their homelands been more favourable, they would certainly not have gambled with their lives and the lives of their loved ones to escape their former existence and take on a totally unknown situation in the New World.

They willingly crossed uncharted oceans in marginally stable sailboats with minimal navigation equipment with whomever they found to be their sea captains. These early people were ambitious, curious, and highly motivated, and they definitely wanted to satisfy the curiosity that had been aroused by the limited information available to them about the New World. They carried hope and optimism in their hearts and minds that they would find a new and better place for themselves and future generations.

These people were aware that the New World would not be a place of ease and relaxation, but they knew how to deal with that. Such knowledge was certainly not allowed to interfere with their goals and ambitions. They wanted a place where they could wrestle a good living out of the environment and they were more than prepared to do whatever was necessary to make this happen. These people worked, and worked, and worked! The New World that we enjoy today is a direct result of the work ethic that came to North America with these people.

In spite of this, all we can do today is be critical of these workers from the past, because we are led to believe that they did not consider adopting the marginal existence that the North American natives endured at the time of their arrival. Such goals and the necessary work ethic had not begun to surface among the natives of Canada because most of them relied completely on nature to maintain their meager existence in their harsh environment.

A major activity that occupied much of the natives' time and limited resources was the primitive tribal wars along every border area of their territories. The new arrivals saw the marginal existence of the majority of the North American natives for what it was. They must have been amazed at what they saw. These people had chosen to leave their homelands and lifestyles, which were far more comfortable in every way than what the natives were living with all across North America.

We should pause and give thanks to our ancestors for the way of life we have the opportunity to enjoy today. This better life is available to all, including the aboriginals. Our ancestors gambled with their lives and worked hard to win their new existence, and we are the beneficiaries.

Today, we as a society look only at the mostly imaginary glory of the native existence as we are taught to believe it was in those pre-invasion times. We buy and display what is said to be native art in wood carvings and totem poles, and promote the mainly false idea of the existence of these things among the natives of long-ago times. The natives were primitive people who lived in teepees or lesser protection from the elements, yet we promote the idea that these people had a wealth of wood and stone carvings and totems which they carried with them in their nomadic existence.

They had no draft animals to assist them in their roaming and had not discovered the wheel. With these facts in mind, we are to believe they added to their burden by possessing wooden and stone artifacts which would hinder their constant mobility in a major way. There were no walls to display these things on, even if they had chosen to haul them. The artistic things we describe as native art may have been part of the culture of some tribal groups, but only in the few locations where these people had a partially fixed location. The majority of the natives would not have added to their struggles in constant relocation by carrying things that were only beneficial from an artistic viewpoint.

New people arrived in ever-increasing numbers, reacting to the limited news that reached their homelands with the crews of returning ships. The people in the Old World were beginning to feel the pressure of their success; their numbers were increasing rapidly and many were beginning to feel a shortage of space and opportunities for themselves, and most certainly for their future generations. Travel to the other side of the world was not a pleasant thought, but their culture and lifestyle and their work ethic had been the cause of their success and many were inclined to look at the move as something akin to their duty to their future generations.

These new people learned that there was a native population in the New World and they must have been amazed to hear the stories of how these people lived. We must consider the thoughts the new immigrants had about the alleged way of life among the North American natives. They could have formed the opinion that they could help the natives improve their primitive lives. There are many examples where their skills could have improved the native existence.

The rumors that reached these potential new settlers while they were still in the Old World were confirmed when they came into contact with the North American natives. This observation is well substantiated when we realistically examine the native living conditions that the new settlers observed and recorded on their arrival in the new territories.

As the influx of foreigners increased, it must have become obvious to anyone who thought about it that the native way of life was no longer viable but was, in fact, in danger. If this observation was made by the natives, then they were obviously not able or willing to adapt to the changes required to take part in the new lifestyle. They were also unwilling or unable to mount any valid defensive action to protect their allegedly cherished lifestyles and cultures we are told of in the modern world.

One of the few obvious activities among the natives following the early arrival of the newcomers was the trapping of every fur-bearing animal they could catch to trade with the newcomers for trinkets and bobbles, blankets and food. The new people who had come as fur traders actively encouraged the natives to bring in furs to the extent that it was well into the 1950s before any beaver were once again sighted along the North Saskatchewan River and its tributaries in Alberta and, no doubt, along every major watershed in Canada. These creatures had been all but exterminated by trapping several hundred years earlier. Traders created the demand but the natives, largely, carried out the extermination.

Today, we are constantly reminded of the respect among the natives for the environment and all the creatures of nature. This constantly-promoted aspect of native existence and culture is difficult to grasp if one considers the trapping overkill and the prairie natives' tradition of stampeding herds of buffalo over cliffs. The natives had learned they could secure vital food by running the buffalo as they did, and while this practice was certainly not one to secure the future of the buffalo herds, the need for food exceeded any thoughts about the well-being of the herds. Piles of bones at the bases of cliffs indicate that this practice had been going on for centuries, but there were still vast buffalo herds when the first traders and settlers arrived on the prairies. Obviously, the buffalo were able to thrive and maintain their numbers in spite of the occasional mass kill on the cliffs.

The accumulation of bones at these massive kill sites took centuries and, therefore, the required numbers in the herds may have taken many years to replenish after every cliff slaughter. The waste of these cliff killings should be given some thought. A small band of natives would suddenly have available the dead and injured carcasses of a great number of buffalo for every man, woman, and child in the perpetrating band. If we give further thought to these cliff killings, we realize that many buffalo would have been only crippled by this barbaric practice and one must wonder how long these surviving creatures were left to suffer among the piles of carcasses below the cliffs. The fact that such mass killings were justified in the natives' minds leads to the conclusion that the crippled animals would simply be left to nature.

Following a tremendous feast, all the perpetrating band of natives could do was migrate to get themselves far away from the horrible stench of many tons of rotting meat. The traditional pemmican made by the natives would have used up another two or three buffalo carcasses before the stench forced them to move on.

The making of pemmican was one of the few activities that the prairie natives learned in their long history in this country, and they should be recognized for the development of this life-preserving practice. Making pemmican had been going on for centuries, or thousands of years, and no doubt was responsible for a better survival rate during the prairie winters that otherwise would have left every tribe with reduced numbers.

My father told me of finding pemmican during land clearing activities on his homestead land near the North Saskatchewan River, about forty miles west of Edmonton. The land clearing work on Dad's farm was started in about 1918 and went on for more than ten years. The pemmican bags consisted of a rawhide bag stuffed full of meat and animal fat along with some vegetation and berries. The bags my father found were mostly from the leg skin of animals, mostly buffalo, the leg having been skinned in the round and the open ends simply folded over the main lump of the pemmican, which was then buried in shallow holes in the ground. Some pemmican balls were formed by folding a flat piece of animal hide over and around the pemmican before it was buried.

The burial practice prevented predators such as wolves, coyotes, and bears from eating them. A thin layer of earth reduces the predatory animals' ability to smell out such choice morsels. No doubt there were markers placed over the burial sites but, obviously, some were not found when the need was there. Alberta winter conditions must have played a large part in the inability of the wintering natives to find some of the buried pemmican, and it remained there for possibly centuries until it was found by land clearing farmers. The vegetation and berries in the pemmican balls would have gone a long way toward preventing diseases due to vitamin shortages.

Chapter 14
Native Reserve System

Americans seem to have instituted the Indian Reserve plan, and it was adopted in Canada, not because it was thought to be good but because it was the only proposal that seemed to have merit in the crisis that both the settlers and the natives faced. The reserve plan offered what appeared to the new people to be a temporary solution for the native situation. If we give some consideration to the background of the new Canadians, with their daring, adventurous, ambitious, and hard-working attitudes, we come to the conclusion that these people looked on the Indian reserve solution as only a stopgap or temporary measure. These new settlers were obviously wrong in their estimation of the aversion to change among the natives.

Many generations have existed in this reserve system and, today, the best efforts of both the natives and the descendants of the new Canadians, tragically, all seem to ensure that this travesty continues. In defense of those from that by-gone era who were faced with the aversion to change and the apparent lack of ambition and work ethic among the natives, the ambitious and hardworking new arrivals to this land could not have foreseen the natives sitting idly on their reserves for centuries.

The reserves were obviously visualized as a temporary situation, to last only until these people got their lives into alignment with the new reality and took up places in the new system of living. These early Canadians were wrong in their assessment of the native aversion to change and work, but they may well have not brought about the reserve system with evil in mind. People who had the ambition, curiosity, and inner drive to bring themselves from the other side of the globe could not imagine some other branch of humanity existing as the natives have done on the reserves for the last 300 or more years. During those same years, thousands of people from nearly every race and culture around the world have taken up residence in North America. Nearly all of these new people abandoned some aspects of their original ways to become good citizens of their adopted land. Few of these people or their descendants have experienced major disadvantages from these huge lifestyle changes.

The natives have adopted a position of completely refusing any changes to their imaginary ideal lifestyles and this attitude is abundant among them today. The position of sympathy and acceptance of the native position in our modern times by great numbers of Canadians has only served to support and encourage these impossible and imaginary goals.

Chapter 15
Primitive Existence

Today, we, as a mainly metropolitan nation, glorify the original native lifestyle in any way our imaginations will allow. We will not accept and propagate the reality that most of the natives lived within the ebb and flow of nature and that they seemed content with this marginal and fluctuating existence. Many of us, along with the natives, who are being coached to some extent, will insist on not looking at the realities of their pre-foreigner existence and the extreme difficulties for any group of people to exist under their chosen but primitive ways. Many of this modern group prefer to pretend that the native existence in those times was all glory and grandness. The reality of these people dying of starvation or freezing to death is something we, in our modern society, flatly refuse to acknowledge, even though there are far more people in Canada today who identify themselves as natives than there were when the first ships arrived from the Old World.

We are being trained to believe that the holes in the ground that some of them spent the Cariboo winters in were nice and comfortable, even though there is ample evidence that the Cariboo was not, even in those pre-white man times, a tropical area. Many natives in the prairie regions of Canada also lived in similar winter accommodations and, undoubtedly, many of them did not live to see the next spring.

Those fortunate natives who occupied the coastal areas of British Columbia and the Maritimes were somewhat better off because of the mild winters and abundant food available from the ocean. These people were better prepared to survive and be ready for the continuous intertribal wars. The mystery along the coastal areas is why there were so few people. The question must come to mind: Why were they not much more numerous in these more ideal living areas? One of the most likely causes of their limited numbers in these ideal locations may be their constant intertribal warfare. With the abundance of easily obtained food, these people would have been able to put much more effort into warfare, and their numbers must have been controlled in this way.

The natives of the British Columbia Cariboo region, along with other tribes in the New World, were more a part of nature than they were trying to cope with it. This fact controlled their numbers, and during the extreme winters of those regions only the strongest would be living when spring arrived. This is one of the primary laws of nature: only the strongest and most determined will survive. It is "survival of the fittest."

The natives were for unknown reasons apparently quite satisfied with this arrangement with nature and they accepted the laws of nature and the constant fluctuations in their survival rates. They must be recognized for their tenacity at the same time as for their inability to construct better winter shelter that would have improved their odds of survival. They would crawl back into the same holes in the ground at the start of the next winter, even though there was a strong possibility that the very young, the old, and the frail or weak would not live to leave those hellish places when spring arrived. These people were not involved in a struggle with nature as was most of humanity; they were much more a part of nature.

If we allow ourselves some analytical thought, we realize that nature is not and never has been the grand provider we are trained to believe it to be. Nature creates food and materials in a great variety of ways, but we must put an abundance of hard work into gathering and preserving of those provisions if we intend to survive over the long haul with only minimal, natural fluctuations in our numbers. The abundant provision by nature will take a different course almost every year. If we do not recognize and record it and do whatever we can to overcome this ebb and flow as a fact of life, then we will experience the same ebb and flow in our numbers, just as the natives did for centuries before the arrival of the new settlers.

Mankind in the Old World developed ways of harnessing nature through agricultural and horticultural methods and they learned to construct buildings that allowed them to survive the natural fluctuations of weather. These struggles with nature over centuries in the Old World, and learning from them, ensured these people's survival in spite of nature and its ebb and flow patterns. There were only a scattered few examples of this type of activity among the natives of North America and almost none on the territory that was to become Canada.

Chapter 16
Basic Vitamin Requirements

A recent news article was about the presence of rickets and scurvy among the children on some northern Manitoba, Saskatchewan, and Alberta native reserves. These natives are among those who live near their traditional lifestyles, yet the children suffer from an illness that is almost unheard of in the modern world. Obviously, the traditional diet of these people would have included the necessary vitamins to prevent this scourge among their children. Their traditional pemmican would have been one of the most reliable sources of basic vitamins; however, modern natives are unwilling or unable to produce this necessity from their original and cherished way of life.

It seems obvious they are no longer willing or able to do the necessary work to gather their traditional food. They have become totally reliant on food shipments from the white world and the foods they prefer are not adequate to prevent this problem. With only a minimal understanding about diet and nutrition, these vitamin deficiency maladies are totally preventable. Taking readily available vitamin capsules a few times each week would eliminate these diseases from their children. Perhaps there should be some organized research done to determine how this anomaly can flourish in the modern world. There are grocery and general stores on these reserves or in nearby communities for the convenience of the residents there.

Natural food sources will, no doubt, be limited; however, they should have the knowledge and ability to feed their children and themselves well enough to prevent scurvy and rickets. The cause of this can be described in two words: junk food. In my years of observing modern native ways, I can verify the overuse of junk food among many of these people. The majority of native mothers I observed continually fed their children with cans or bottles of soft drinks along with bags of potato chips and chocolate bars. Neither the young natives nor any other youth from any background would pass up this sort of food in favour of pemmican or dried wild berries, even if some of the older tribe members had taken the trouble to provide such life sustaining food. An occasional meal of pemmican or fruit from the local store is all that is required to keep scurvy and rickets at bay. Circumstances such as these are difficult to blame on the early settlers or their descendants. It appears the fault lies with the natives alone.

Today we are constantly reminded of the natives' great respect for their culture. Progress would come to all of us, native and others, if someone were to investigate and write a detailed account of exactly what "native culture" is and was. The term is left open for each person to form their own definition of this vague thing, a situation that allows generalities in spoken or written information. The modern-day people of both native and other ancestry are led to believe that "native culture" consisted of only positive and grand things, yet none of these things are clearly documented for the benefit of those of us who may think and question any aspect of it. There must also be some aspects of "native culture" that are not grand and positive, such as the constant intertribal wars, inadequate modes of shelter, and the frequent loss of friends and family by starvation or exposure. These tragedies should also be considered a part of "culture," along with the inability and unwillingness to try to make improvements in their pre-foreigner existence.

The hard facts of their pre-invasion existence made it difficult for the natives to take a hard and fast stand on how and where to deal with the traders and settlers as they began to appear. The natives could plainly see that the new people practiced many methods and improvements over the way they had existed forever. Had their pre-invasion existence been anything like they have been led to believe over the centuries since the invasion, they would have had much less of a problem deciding whether to oppose the newcomers on every front or to simply stand by and watch it happen, in the way they all did.

The natives only began to oppose the invasion after about 200 years had passed, with ambush attacks on settlers and workers. An example of this slow response is the Chilcotin native attack on a road construction crew in the coastal mountains of British Columbia. Thirteen road construction workers were shot and killed by a group of seven Chilcotin natives as they worked on a road through the Homathco River valley to the Cariboo gold fields. This slaughter would seem to have been more for vengeance than for defense or protection of their territory and their allegedly cherished way of life. Seven Chilcotin men were rounded up over the months following the ambush and five of them were later hanged for their part in it.

Chapter 17
Modern Misunderstanding of Nature

Our scholarly leaders and teachers of today are fully convinced of the kind and wonderfully generous provisions of nature. They have been learning this fallacy for generations and few question this established "fact." Every child growing up in a rural setting on the Canadian prairie fifty to 100 years ago observed nature in ways that city dwelling people are not aware of in our unnatural world of today. The vision of a predator eating the entrails of a still-living creature does not bring about thoughts of the grand and wonderful ways of nature. They have not experienced the sight of an overpopulation of nature's creatures freezing and starving to death because their natural, uncontrolled numbers had eaten all their food supply and nature had provided the mange parasite that caused these doomed creatures to slough off their winter coats during some of the most severe prairie winter conditions. The sight of crows and magpies raiding the nests of smaller birds and dropping the immature young birds on the ground where they slowly starved to death was also and still is a part of nature.

These things are a real part of nature and they come with the wonderful and generous provision of food and shelter that nature provides for all of creation only when the environment is favourable. There are many wonderful aspects to nature, but it is far short of the grand and benevolent provider described to the up-and-coming citizens in our civilized and unnatural world of today.

Beautiful phrases and descriptions like "Old Mother Nature" and "Let nature take its course" and similar buzzwords generate a false picture of this miraculous thing. Nature can be vicious and deadly at one moment and the provider of all the necessities of life at the next.

We should think about this before we continue to propagate this faulty information. Nature is a wonderful thing, but "kindness" and "caring provision" are definitely not a part of its regular vocabulary. Great good frequently comes from nature, but so do harsh things. If mankind is not prepared to make do with alternatives, they will perish at the whim of nature, just as all other creatures will within its control. Modern civilizations have flourished in most instances because citizens have learned to "make do" and they have learned to work hard to preserve a food supply and construct adequate shelter.

These actions in most applications have been contrary to the overall ways of nature. The new pioneers brought these "work and make do" skills and experience with them and applied this knowledge willingly and vigorously to their new environment. The methods and skills and hard work needed to guarantee a living were clearly demonstrated to the natives of those times; however, it seems few of them were of a mind to learn and apply these sometimes difficult practices. The majority seemed to prefer their past methods wherein they simply took what nature provided, as did all the other creatures of the unspoiled wilderness, and they seemed to be prepared to accept death as the cost of this practice when nature failed them. These attitudes among the natives may have been based on superstition or religious beliefs that did not allow for actions contrary to nature's way.

The overpopulation of our world today is cause for disturbing thoughts along this line. If all of humanity had been prepared to live within the whims and cycles of nature as the natives seemed to be, the world would not be facing the overpopulation problems of today. I will leave that for someone else to write about.

Chapter 18
Origin of the Residential Schools

The evil of the residential school plan is abundantly displayed for all to appreciate in our modern world. We should take a break from this programmed thinking and give a moment of unbiased thought to the real reasons our government of those long ago times deliberately assembled such a thing. We do not need an expensive judicial inquiry to conclude that the settlers and their leaders during those times had more to do with their time than to unnecessarily interfere with the lifestyles of the natives. They were more than just a little bit busy wrestling their own living from difficult circumstances in those early years. There was no government bureaucracy or police force or even a standing military during the outset of this educational program in 1831. There had to be a significant motivating factor to bring these busy, financially challenged, democratically inclined people to attempt such a tremendous undertaking. What could possibly have been in their minds?

In spite of the current and deliberately programmed mindset among the media and our politicians, I believe we can all be certain that these people did not see an urgent need to force the native people into their way of thinking and doing. The ugly facts are more likely that these early Canadians were seeing unimaginable things happening at most of the native settlements. They could not bring themselves to leave such mismanagement and gross neglect of children to continue without some attempt to assist. Perhaps it was the sight of barefooted native children running around in the snow or a drunken young native's body frozen solid around the stump of a tree, or small children being neglected and allowed to play on a railway bridge until a train chopped them to pieces.

Or perhaps it was the house fire on a totally drunken potlatching interior reserve where two little boys died because they were playing with matches in their unsupervised home while their little sister ran cross-country to try to get help from a nearby ranch. The rancher's wife who answered the frantic knocking at her door could see the glow of fire in the sky as the little girl told her of her most recent experience with gross neglect. The little girl knew there was not a hope in hell of finding help in her own community. She had lived there all her life and was certain there was not an adult in the entire reserve village capable of assisting her in controlling the dangerous play of her younger brothers. During the burning of the house, the wild and out-of-control drunken partying continued in several nearby houses.

Another horror witnessed on several interior reserves was the sight of neglected, diapered children playing under street lights at two o'clock in the morning; in some places, they were exposed to the dangers of vehicle traffic. These are only a few of the horrible things I have witnessed during my police career, and I am sure that similar sights were abundant in the native settlements before the residential school system was attempted.

Obviously, with our modern knowledge and an abundance of hindsight, the residential schools were not the correct or proper method to apply to such a situation, but they were perhaps the best that the limited skills and resources were able to conceive under the circumstances of those times. We must bear in mind that the residential school system was established from coast to coast in

Canada. Many people gave consideration and thought to this thing and to a number of alternatives, but it was brought about anyway. There must have been great motivational force on these early people with far more important needs than their desire to change the general conduct of the natives and their culture only to make them conform to the settlers' standards.

The situation on many reserves was beyond the imaginations of the new people, even during the non-drinking times. No doubt alcohol intoxication of the population of some communities would have swayed the thoughts of the decision-makers and brought them to realize that something had to be done and it had to be done immediately.

The modern description of the original native situation in our world today consists of a glorious home life for all these children, with caring, sober parents constantly involved with educating their children about their "culture" and lifestyles. Many of us have accepted this fallacy without much thought. We are led to believe that the evil bastards who invaded the almost flawless native lifestyles and cultures simply decided they must break up these native families and force their religion and lifestyle on them. This course of action was decided on even in the face of the unending work the invaders were faced with to procure the necessities of life for themselves.

The family unit has always been valued in every human society. We are now asked to believe that the early decision-makers of our society simply chose to destroy all these families to force the native population to comply with their methods and wishes. Can we get to the point where we will thoughtfully and rationally believe that? Our early ancestors on their homesteads all across Canada were involved in the struggle for their own survival and to improve their daily existence; they were busy with the task of wrestling their own existence from nature. They were not concerned with the native lifestyle unless the concern was forced on them by the obvious plight of the natives and, especially, the native children.

The residential schools served two purposes, the most obvious to take the native children out of the horrible conditions the settlers and decision-makers witnessed every day. The second purpose was to bring education and a changed attitude to these young people.

In reality, the people in authority in those times were faced with a totally new and unbelievable situation. The natives conducted themselves in a way that was beyond what those people could comprehend. The conditions on the reserves must have been beyond belief for such a drastic plan to have been hatched and financed. Early Canadians were financially challenged beyond what we can imagine today. Then, in the midst of a time when these new people were almost totally involved in the struggle to maintain and improve their own existence in the harsh realities of their recently adopted land, we are asked to accept that they would undertake a project as large as the residential schools from coast to coast.

Today, we are taught that the settlers and their appointed leaders had nothing more important to do with their time and energy than to force their values and methods on the natives. If we give this some unbiased thought, we must conclude that the new settlers had more pressing things to do with their time and effort in their chosen area of what was largely an uncivilized place. Today, all we do for the decision-makers of those times is vigorously condemn everything they fought for in their genuine hope of improving the overall situation for these people and their future generations. They had limited resources and they were faced with a staggering problem, which, in their rational minds, could not be allowed to continue. What they saw demanded immediate action. They did not choose to be cruel and overpowering in their actions; they simply could not allow these horrendous situations to continue among these people without attempting corrective action. There were exceptions to this situation in some places, but this ugly reality must have been overpowering to our ancestors in almost every native settlement, and they felt they were being forced to generate corrective action.

The instigation of the residential school system must have been tremendously expensive at a time when there was little money for any sort of government action or program. There would have been vigorous opposition to it even in those long-ago times, yet it happened because of the unbelievable situations that prevailed on most of the native settlements. Only a few of the horrendous sights I saw among the natives in my growing up on the Canadian prairie and my years of policing in the British Columbia interior have been mentioned.

There were many other shocking and unbelievable events that I am quite sure did not have their origin in the much-maligned native residential school system. These horrors came about entirely because of the conduct and attitude abundant among the natives. The trend today is to lay the blame for all negative native behaviour on the residential schools, although there are now many natives in the local reserve government systems who did not attend these reportedly evil establishments. Even so, the evidence of misappropriation and theft is abundant. With the continuation of the current trends to blame the new people for every aspect of the native situation, we will now be asked to assume that the alleged damage from the residential schools is hereditary and will no doubt account for such behaviour for many coming generations.

The most overwhelming reason for the establishment of the residential school system will have been the native weakness or, perhaps, their allergic reaction to the effects of alcohol. The laid-back, take it as it comes attitude of the natives is also a contributing factor, but in a much lesser way. Some semblance of order and acceptable conduct can always be brought about and enforced by government programs, as long as the people involved are not insane and are sober for the majority of the time.

This situation, in regard to drinking, was not the rule among the natives during their earliest encounters with alcohol, and this has not diminished much over the last 300 years. The natives have displayed what could be accurately described as an allergic reaction to alcohol since their first experiences with this substance. Alcohol is all-powerful over the mind and conduct of the natives in almost every situation, a reaction that is not confined to the natives alone. Many among us are unable to deal with the effects of alcohol consumption and the cost and damage to our modern population is immeasurable. The weaknesses among the natives to the effects of alcohol were documented in the early records of the first foreigners who had experience where this substance first became available to these people.

In a recent public information document, it was suggested that the native weakness to alcohol came about from the evils of the residential school system. Contrary to this theory, however, is the fact that this alcohol intolerance was documented in our early history, at least 100 years before the first residential school existed.

The alcohol problem among the natives has brought about some strange laws and regulations. As non-native populations gradually increased across Canada and communities were established with licensed liquor outlets or government liquor stores, the natives were prohibited from entering these places. Such a law is obviously a racially discriminating action; such a race-based program could not be considered under any circumstances in Canada today. The reason for this harsh and discriminatory law must be realistically looked at. Obviously, the inability of the majority of the natives to deal with the effects of alcohol consumption was the primary reason for such action but today, it is being falsely played back to us as having been exclusively for the purpose of abuse and discrimination against this identifiable minority.

There may have been a racist motivation among a few of the decision-makers of those times; however, the native conduct and their obvious inability to cope with the powerful effects of this substance played the major part in the origin of such law. As a young person growing up on the Canadian prairies, I clearly recall an expression used to describe the actions of a person from any racial background who could not or would not control their consumption of alcohol. They were described as having "gone Indian." This expression was understood among the early settlers, as most of them would have been witness to many incidents where this phenomenon was displayed by their native neighbours.

One positive aspect of this questionable legislative action by the dominant society is that the lives of some natives have been saved by it.

Time changes all things; the natives have been allowed access to liquor for many years, but their control of it is still in much need of improvement. Abstinence does not seem to be a viable method. The natives from most of Canada have learned some unusual and odd methods of dealing with alcohol. In most places, the natives have found that the alcohol most suited to their "all-out binge" drinking style are beer and wine, with emphasis on wine. Hard liquor, or distilled liquor, in any of its many forms, can be deadly in an all-out binge because the blood alcohol level of the drinker rises so rapidly that it frequently causes sudden death by alcohol shock. This tragic fact has been demonstrated by many young people, both native and non-native, during their first experiments with liquor. These events all too frequently resulted in a police officer having to go to the door of some family member to advise that a healthy and strong young person will never be coming home again.

Beer or wine will seldom if ever produce such a result. The consumption of great quantities of these products over a short period of time often causes the over-eager drinker to vomit. This uncontrollable purging reaction almost always saves his or her life. Many Canadian natives have learned this lesson through constant and dedicated practice. Another positive point for wine consumption, from the native point of view, is cost. The largest volume of the active ingredient can be obtained for each dollar spent if the purchase is cheap wine.

Chapter 19
Missing Women Inquiries

Today, many of our highly paid politicians, police leaders, and native leaders cry for another detailed and expensive investigation into the many native girls and women who have been murdered or disappeared and are then, logically, assumed to have been murdered.

Having lived a large part of my life near a variety of native communities in Alberta and British Columbia, I do not see a need for another expensive and politically motivated inquiry. The causes of almost all of these tragedies are obvious. We, like most freedom-based societies, have criminals and perverts among us in abundance. All these criminal scum need is an opportunity. They travel the roads with a stash of liquor and/or drugs on the pathetically frequent chance that an opportunity will present itself. The native girls and women of Canada are, tragically, the leading source of these opportunities.

This situation has no single and simple solution. We could attempt legislation that would forbid criminals and perverts from lurking about native areas or from driving vehicles along our highways, but the ineffectiveness of this should be abundantly obvious without the need for a lot of analytical thought or another expensive judicial inquiry. Common sense must, therefore, tell us that the lessening of these tragic events must be started among those who are the most common victims. There are a great number of things that this victim group could and should change in their current conduct to bring about a reduction in these horrible statistics.

The most willfully overlooked fact in these horrible statistics is alcohol and the abundant abuse of it. Women are vulnerable in many ways in our modern, open society where criminals are frequently allowed to take advantage of their rights over others. A woman alone on a dark city street or in an isolated, rural setting is in obvious danger. A drunken woman in any of the same locations is away beyond that description. It has been said that a lone drunken woman in almost any location is "asking for" trouble. This tragic fact applies equally to native women and any others as well.

A detailed statistical examination of the missing and murdered native women shows the use and abuse of alcohol or drugs by the majority of these victims. What is most needed is for the politicians and native leaders to sit down and discuss these events in a straight-forward and honest way. Such discussions must begin by looking at the actual facts—the way things are, not as we wish or pretend things to be. These discussions must begin after politicians put aside their fear of losing votes or popularity or hurting feelings, and the natives have taken an unbiased look at all the statistical data available about these tragedies. People are dying almost daily for no valid reason, but the majority of our politicians and the native leaders are doing little to change this tragic situation. The main reason they are doing nothing is because they lack the determination and guts to face the ugly facts and to call for realistic and factual discussions of the entire matter. As long as our politicians, the native leaders, and our media people are unwilling or unable to talk about the actual facts, this travesty will continue and native women will continue to be the obvious majority in these tragic numbers.

Another willfully overlooked fact is that approximately 70 percent of the native women who have been murdered in Canada were killed by other natives. The tragic, totally uncaring attitude among many natives is the main factor in these statistics, but there is little or no indication that these people are prepared to do something about it. There are some among the native communities who understand these facts; however, they seem to be more prepared to lay blame on the white society than to grapple with the ugly situation and bring about some corrective action where it would be most effective.

Chapter 20
No-Win Situation

The majority of the natives of Canada today are caught up in a no-win situation unless they pull themselves out of the quagmire that has been created for them and by them over the history of their involvement with the newcomers. Almost all the programs and policies that have come about over the past many years have served only to guarantee a marginalized place in Canadian society for the natives.

The residential school system was undoubtedly harsh and cruel; however, it can be argued that this program was more productive and beneficial than many other programs put forward before and since that time. Tragically, the majority of Canadian natives have become confused by these mistakes and errors in judgment by the dominant Canadian society in general and those of their own doing. Many of today's natives have an overwhelming feeling of victimization and, therefore, entitlement.

These feelings have been spawned within the native societies by our failed attempts to deal with their problems while carefully avoiding common sense. Great effort has been put forth to avoid actually looking at and trying to deal with the ugly realities of life and human history. Human societies, cultures, and nations have been overtaken or overrun by others since the beginning of time, a situation that was not uncommon between warring native tribes in North America. The only mode of survival for the losers in these cruel events was to adapt to the world as it was available to them or as it was left available to them.

This unfortunate turn of fate has been dealt with by nearly every race of humanity at some time in their history. Close examination of any of these defeated people would no doubt show that none of the survivors of these great injustices waited for 300 years, or more than fifteen generations, before taking corrective action.

The ancient Chinese philosophy of Tao has many facets, among which is the common sense belief that for every action undertaken by humanity there is an equal and opposite reaction. There are two or more sides to every situation. This ancient belief clearly states that only by looking at all sides of a situation can we come to a judgment or decision that will be as close as possible to being fair or beneficial to all involved parties.

In recent times, mass media and most everyone in authority over such things have put great effort into misleading the Canadian population about the causes of the plight of the Canadian natives. We have only been made aware of what appear to be, or what has been embellished to make it appear to be, positive aspects of the natives and their history. The actions, conduct, and behaviour of the majority of Canadian natives over recent generations have contributed to their current situation; therefore, by only looking at one side of their sad predicament, we are undoubtedly prolonging these difficulties into future generations.

The present-day Canadian native is now the fifteenth or possibly the twentieth generation since their sad experience with the new arrivals to this country. The necessary process of adapting themselves to the world as it is now has been neglected by the natives for far too long. This will be a difficult transition for most of the native population; however, a more realistic look at the world today will clearly show that there is no viable alternative.

The right to hunt and fish and live as hunter-gatherers is of little value to these people today. The acceptance of Canada and the world as it is today will be a long and slow process for the Canadian natives. This tragic fact has been clearly demonstrated in the past 300 years of their history; however, if the process is not started soon, it will be another 300 years, or fifteen or twenty more wasted generations for these people.

The original way of life for these people is gone. Despite the effort to pretend it is still possible and doable, that life can exist only in dreams. The natives of today are born into a totally different world than the one their ancestors were born into 300 or more years ago. The finding of fault on the part of the natives of those times or on the part of the settlers who chose to enter into the struggle to make a living in the New World will not make the situation better for either of the parties involved in this tragedy. The world is a different place today. The native way of existence is no longer possible and no amount of pretending or complaining will alter that fact. If we look realistically at the situations of today, we will see that the natives themselves are not willing or able to go back to their old existence, even if this were possible.

There are still native populations in some of the more isolated areas of Canada living as near as possible to their former ways; however, without regular money and food supplements from the dominant society, none of these isolated groups would survive on a permanent basis. If they were left to the natural cycles of nature, which they claim as an important part of their culture, there would be unacceptable fluctuations in their numbers. The cycles of the altered nature of today will force these people to rely on the dominant society for the necessities of life and some measure of comfort during the down cycles of nature. In their original way of life and survival, the results of the frequent down cycles in nature were obvious. Their populations were controlled by nature. The compassionate attitude of modern Canada will guarantee that whatever can be done for people in such circumstances will be done. Filling the basic needs of these isolated native groups will certainly not be neglected in our society today. Such actions are contrary to nature, and the natives tell us that they are prepared to live by the rules and regulations of nature, even though they do not, cannot, and will not.

Chapter 21
Police Are Always Wrong

In the very civilized Western world of today, it is fashionable to be extremely critical of those who serve the public as police officers. The native citizens of Canada have long claimed that they were frequently the subjects of organized and willful acts of discrimination by the Canadian population through their police forces. Those of us who have served as police officers over the years have also been subjected to various forms of discrimination and can, therefore, understand more fully the mindsets of many of our native citizens.

Leaders in our society recently appointed some justice officials to delve into a detailed re-examination of the work done by various police agencies on the British Columbia lower mainland surrounding the investigation of the hideous and unimaginable crimes of Willie Picton. At the risk of displaying a questionable attitude about the Picton re-examination, it should be stated that the result of the inquiries appears to have been determined before the first word of evidence was recorded. The obvious purpose of the inquiry was only to gather evidence to support the established contention that the police had not done a proper job of the investigation.

Willie Picton was a worker/owner on a family farm operation in Coquitlam, British Columbia, where he was described as a pig farmer. Picton was eventually convicted of a number of murders, wherein he picked up street prostitutes in Vancouver and took them to his nearby farm in Coquitlam, where they were used and then murdered by unimaginable methods.

The number of missing person reports directed mainly to the Vancouver City Police were a clear indication that some person or persons were likely involved in the systematic disappearance of these women. The fact that no bodies were found was a large factor in the doubts that surrounded this case. The mystery of the missing bodies was solved at a later time through laboratory processes on samples of soil and debris from the Picton pig farm.

Willie Picton was definitely not just an ordinary hateful individual. He should be remembered as one of the most despicable pieces of excrement humanity has spawned. The majority of Picton's victims were native Indian women, a fact that did not make the frequent disappearances a truly unusual event. The percentage of native women among the street prostitutes in that part of Vancouver may be similar to the percentage of Picton's victims, who were of native ancestry. Picton may have deliberately selected obviously native victims; however, there is also a strong possibility that he simply targeted street prostitutes.

Many will interpret the faltering start of the police investigation into the Picton crimes as a sign of racist, uncaring attitudes toward natives, and particularly the native women who act as street prostitutes. This fact and mindset among some police officers may have contributed to the slow start to the initial investigation of these crimes, but it was a long way from being the main factor. Contrary to the modern attitude about them, it must be pointed out that the police are restricted in their abilities to speculate about crime or even the lack of it. The infatuation among the modern public about their rights to privacy and secrecy means the police must have a fairly solid case before they are allowed to ask simple questions.

The native women who frequent the seedy parts of Canadian cities are a nomadic group. They come and go from their often remote home areas or simply drift away into some other, similar situation in another city. An examination of the statistics about the many reports of missing street women will shed some light on these facts.

The outcry from grieving families and friends of these missing women resulted in the appointment of a group of judiciary officials to do a thorough examination of the actions of the police following the reports of the missing native women later found to have become Picton's victims. The cost of this inquiry should have been a matter of public record; however, if there was ever a mention of these costs in the public media, they were certainly not given much coverage.

The Picton investigation spawned another call for similar inquiries about missing native women in the mid-Canada area and along the highway between Prince George and Prince Rupert in central British Columbia. These areas of concern should justify another in-depth questioning about the actions of the police in every area where a native woman has disappeared.

There may be justification for some corrective actions in the police response but, tragically, there is often little for the police to work with. The current Canadian mindset is such that the police are expected to work miracles at the outset of every such incident. The police find themselves without verifiable information that could support the suspicion that foul play has occurred. The frequency of these reports of missing native women also adds to the lack of credibility of these reports.

The grieving family who reports their loved one having not contacted them for an unusual period of time will tell the police all they know about the subject. She has frequented the skid row area of several major cities in the recent past; she drinks excessively, is a frequent user of drugs, and acts as a street prostitute to finance her chosen lifestyle. She often travels by hitchhiking and has told many scary stories of what seemed to be close calls at the hands of some person who picked her up on the streets or highways.

These ugly facts are of no comfort to worried family members, but there is almost nothing to establish a footing for a police investigation. The sad fact is that almost every police organization in every major Canadian city will receive a missing person report similar to this one almost every day. Where should the police investigation begin? Should there not be some community action among the native populations to stop or lessen this dangerous conduct among their own people? The problem is not a new one and such a course of action will do nothing for the families of those who are now on the missing person lists, but it would be a beginning point for some positive action among the natives themselves.

The scenario described is not a perfect fit in every case of a missing native woman, but it is tragically accurate in the majority. There have been too many tragic events along Canadian highways and in the seedy parts of our major cities, and the majority of these tragedies involve young native women. One would expect that anyone could drive from coast to coast in Canada without seeing a single female person "thumbing" for a ride, but this is not the case. They are still out there and the majority appear to be of native ancestry.

What could the police and the population at large do to more accurately portray such an activity as extremely dangerous and particularly so if you are a woman? Our roads and highways are frequented by most or many of our worst perverts, who constantly watch for their next victim as they travel. These despicable individuals have had experience in this ugly area of life in a totally open society and they know well how to take advantage of what is presented to them by a hitchhiking native woman. They will make it their business to have a stash of liquor and/or drugs with them in the event that a victim presents herself for their sick pleasure. If the victim willingly accepts the offer of liquor or drugs, the remainder of the event is tragically obvious, with the only question being if she is finally dumped at the roadside alive or as a corpse.

Every free and open society such as ours will have a number of these dirt bags who will not pass up an opportunity to pick up another victim. There are no methods of eliminating these things and there are not enough funds available to police the roads and highways to make it safe for hitchhiking activity by women. The only option available at this time is for everyone, but women in particular, to not do that!

Chapter 22
Truth Commission

As I write of this tragic story, the Truth Commission is deep into their re-examination of the alleged atrocities in recent history by the staff, the police, and the casual workers at the many Canadian native residential schools. An elderly native witness at a British Columbia hearing testified to the Truth Commission of her clear recollections of being beaten into unconsciousness nearly every night of her years at a residential school. The beatings were alleged to have been inflicted by the teachers and staff, and she also remembered being shot at and wounded by shotgun fire from the same people when she tried to run away. This witness told that these atrocious events happened during her childhood as a student in one of the native residential schools in Canada in the 1970s. The testimony provided by this witness was reported in the news, and details were placed on the Internet for the world to see and appreciate. The Internet world, and most Canadians, now have a new and amazing story about mind boggling cruelty in Canada during relatively recent times.

This type of story will certainly damage any proud feelings among our young citizens and will go a long way toward changing the feelings of those of us who have considerable time invested in Canadian citizenry. This story, presented under oath, leaves an audience to believe that Canada is a place where children were beaten into unconsciousness on a regular basis and deadly force was used to prevent escape, and that these barbaric practices

Charles Scheideman

were prevalent and condoned as recently as the end of the 1970s. Another facet of this horrible conduct is that it was allegedly done in government-financed and church-run school establishments.

The accuracy of the memories of this witness and many others should have been thoroughly examined prior to their giving evidence, and most definitely during the presentation, if the pre-examination was not acceptable. Assuming that this person's recall of those times is accurate, and there is every indication that it was judged to be so, there should be a detailed examination of the written records and memories of everyone who is still available to determine how such sub-human conduct could have been perpetrated in Canada at any time in our history, but especially during recent times.

At this time, I am unaware of any attempt to find survivors from the staff and workers at any of these schools to verify or deny allegations by witnesses such as this woman. There seems to be no desire among the staff of the Truth Commission to hear and learn what some of these people would testify to. They seem to be completely convinced that all the information they will need for their in-depth research will be available and obtained exclusively from the former native students.

The fact that all these witnesses will be eligible for considerable new "hand-out" compensation does not seem to influence or even enter the overall picture. The established mindset of these commissioners seems to have been firm even before the first witness was heard. Perhaps this is hindsight; however, the Truth Commission should give some thought to the native witness from Burns Lake, British Columbia, who recently testified about sexual abuse against herself by one of the residential school teachers. Many questions from the defense finally brought about an investigation, which proved that this witness had not attended that school. Following this startling discovery, the other three witnesses failed to appear to further their claims of sexual abuse, a fact that raises strong questions in my suspicious mind. The Truth Commission should be reconvened to do some of their in-depth inquiries into the conduct and testimony of these witnesses from Burns Lake.

Many valid questions arise from the stories presented to the Truth Commission by this witness, yet it seems quite clear that no one involved in the hearings took the unpopular responsibility of seeking the answers.

1) What methods and screening processes were applied in the finding and hiring of staff for these evil establishments and what motivated these chosen, and in many cases well-educated, employees to commit criminal acts and to use deadly force against defenseless children on a regular and routine basis?

2) What methods were in place to prevent basic human decency from rising to the surface in just one of the great number of persons who came to these schools to earn a living and practice their chosen profession as a school teacher or child counsellor? Surely there would have been some persons somewhere in such a vast system who would not have continually and deliberately overlooked the daily torture and criminal abuse of children.

3) Were the many native and part-native employees of these schools also totally in support of the barbaric treatments this witness tells us were routinely perpetrated against defenseless children?

4) Where were the firearms obtained from and who was responsible for the issue of weapons and ammunition to the teachers and their support staff

at these schools? What policies were in place to compel these people to carry and use firearms for such a heinous purpose?

5) Where was the training in firearms proficiency conducted prior to issuing arms and ammunition to previously inexperienced school teachers and child counsellors? Canadian law required such training and control even in those long-ago times.

6) Were the many native and Metis employees of these schools also issued firearms for use against these defenseless children to prevent their desperate attempts to escape?

7) The alleged use of firearms by inexperienced people to prevent escape by these children must have resulted in fatalities in a few incidents. Firearms are inclined to contribute to such things, and much more so if they are in the hands of only marginally trained and inexperienced people. The dead body of a child who had been shot would have resulted in the unavoidable need for an inquest by the local coroner. Questions would have been raised and there would have been no justifiable answers.

8) All of the reported atrocities took place a long time before the Canadian Charter of Rights had been proclaimed, but most Canadian citizens, even in those times, had a deep understanding of proper and justifiable conduct. Why did not a single person come forward to the police or other authorities at just one of the many school locations across the nation to report such flagrant and life-endangering abuse of defenseless children?

9) All of the residential schools were at least partially operated and controlled by people from the many

Christian churches across Canada. This fact may have brought some individuals into contact with these defenseless children who should definitely not have been in such a position of trust; however, there will have been a far greater number of these church people who were dedicated to their responsibilities and their calling. We are being asked to believe that not one of these people from all the schools across Canada saw fit to report some aspect of this horrible child abuse to the police or any other authorities. Any policemen who worked during those times will have no doubt whatever that the police, anywhere in this country, would have investigated any reports of such sub-human conduct, even if the alleged victims had not been children.

On June 2, 2015, the Canada-wide Truth and Reconciliation Commission released their report after six years of interviewing former students of the residential schools. These institutions existed across Canada for 165 years, from 1831 until 1996.

The investigation was under the supervision of Mr. Justice Murray Sinclair, a man with a long-standing reputation in the Canadian justice system. Mr. Sinclair became a qualified lawyer in 1979 in the province of Manitoba. His career advanced in the Canadian justice system until he became a judge of the Court of Queen's Bench for Manitoba in 2001. Justice Sinclair has worked throughout his lifetime and has been successful and dedicated to the system of justice in Canada. He is also a native Indian. His parents and grandparents were students in the residential school system in Canada, a fact that should have been a large incentive to him in conducting these years of inquiries and interviews.

In researching the history of the Truth and Reconciliation Commission, the name and history of another western Canadian lawyer came to the fore. This man is Wilton Littlechild, who was born and raised on the Ermineskin Reservation in Alberta, where he is presently the chief. He has enjoyed a long and prosperous law career; he was the federal member of Parliament for the Alberta riding of Wetaskiwan-Rimby from 1988 to 1993. His constituents were a general cross-section of Canadians from that central Alberta area.

Neither this man nor Justice Sinclair could be cited as an example of racial discrimination in Canada; on the contrary, they should be viewed as two successful Canadian men. These two men made the decision many years ago to live in, and make the most of, the world they were both born into.

There has been a great deal of expensive work done by the members of the Truth and Reconciliation Commission over the six years they have been engaged in this huge task. Their report is detailed in every area of the tragic history of the residential schools wherever this history displays possibly harmful aspects for the native students.

Mr. Littlechild was a student in these residential schools for fourteen years of his early childhood. As a youth, after completing his high school there, he then moved on to the University of Alberta where he continued his studies and became a lawyer. The traumatic experience of these evil schools did not seem to have caused permanent damage to this man as it is said to have done to nearly every other native student who attended one.

There is another story of a young native girl who was a student in one or several of these places, where she excelled in her studies. She received encouragement from the dedicated staff at her schools and went on to become a Canadian registered nurse. I am sure there are a considerable number of other native children who received their education from one of these places and went on to a successful life. There is an obvious one-sided slant on the Truth and Reconciliation Commission report that has been tragically common to every native inquiry in recent Canadian history.

We are now experiencing pressure to hold another inquiry into the records of the many missing and murdered native women and girls across the nation. If this comes to reality, there should be some harsh and direct thought into the purpose and conduct of the investigation. If it follows the path of most of the recent, similar inquisitions, the outcome will be obvious before the first witness is heard. A complete detailed record of every real or imagined error or omission by a police officer in connection with a missing native woman will be of little or no use in dealing with the basic causes of these tragedies. However, if the current trends continue, the detailed recording of such a list will be the entire function of the next inquiry. The conduct of the many victims of these tragedies will not be dealt with because such things are not spoken about in modern, politically correct Canada. Only information that is, or can be, embellished to appear as a positive aspect for these people will be allowed to be recorded.

Chapter 23
Native Financial Corruption

The recent events at Attawapiskat are only a few examples of the inability among our native people to deal with financial matters on a large scale. A similar fraud and corruption case can be pointed out among almost every tribal leadership group in this country. The ongoing aftermath of Attawapiskat demonstrates that the majority of native Indians of Canada appear to not see any fault with the conduct of their leaders, regardless of the evidence of fraud, corruption, and favouritism.

Information made available to the Canadian public indicates there is still widespread support among the Attawapiskat tribe members for the woman who had somehow become their leader. This person has not been charged criminally or even asked to step down from her position as chief, a clear indication that her loyal subjects are prepared to support her in future similar acts. The information made available to the Canadian public indicated that the Attawapiskat band had received enough government money in this case to make a tremendous difference in the terrible poverty that was and is still prevalent among the citizens of this place. The great mystery of Attawapiskat is this continued support from the people who were systematically robbed by this woman and her cohorts.

In similar non-native situations, these people would be in danger from any number of their constituency. Why are all these people prepared to support this person as their leader and why did the police investigation not lead to numerous criminal charges against the chief and her cohorts? The funds were traceable until they came into the hands of the chief and her cohorts. From that point, there was nothing but missing funds, misery, and mystery. Those of us who have experience and knowledge of the modern police situation will understand that there may have been police recommendations for criminal charges; however, such suggestions must first be cleared by our crown-appointed lawyers, and these people are under the influence of a strong and imposing set of standards in regard to what is politically correct or incorrect.

Attawapiskat received more press attention than similar stories, perhaps because so many reserve residents were cold and hungry at the same time their leaders were wallowing in excess money and resources. There is little room for doubt that there were attempts among politicians and bureaucrats to keep this thing out of the public eye; however, it was just too big to hide. Chief Spence and her cohorts obviously let greed and criminal actions take the place of common sense and decency, but when the smoke had cleared, they got away with it! Who are the "dumb guys" here?

An interesting thing about the television news broadcasts during the Attawapiskat crisis was the brief view of a recent model of a high-end Chevrolet pick-up truck lying with its four wheels in the air somewhere in the midst of the general squalor of the reserve. It seems the reporters and their assistants from the two major Canadian television networks were unable to see this thing, or they simply did not see any significance to it being there. The fact that there are almost no usable roads around this place and that there are only ice roads into this place during a few months of the winter should have piqued some interest in such an anomaly. The vision was transmitted for Canadians by a third television producer, but without comment about the presence of this thing at that place. It was indeed interesting to note that only one television producer saw fit to make even this brief glimpse available to the Canadian television news-watching population. It is abundantly obvious that such a negative image about our natives is beneath the two main television providers, or they are subjected to a strict set of rules that require deep thought and careful consideration before presenting such a vision to the Canadian taxpaying population at large.

Perhaps their need for the continuation of the huge subsidies of our money had some sway on the decisions by our two main television producers to not show this image. The third television producer was obviously under some pressure to only depict views that fit the Canadian standards for such things. However, they did slip a brief television shot of this thing into their broadcast. I am unaware of any inquiry about the source or purpose of this luxury vehicle at that place. The retail cost, or even the tax-exempt cost, of such a vehicle would have gone a long way toward reducing the misery of the people there. News from the same third Canadian television source also tells us that Chief Spence drives a Cadillac Escalade, obviously a more suitable vehicle for a person of such great importance and mass income from her prestigious employment.

The third Canadian television provider was *Sun News*, headquartered in Toronto, Ontario. We, as true Canadians, were not encouraged to watch this programming because, we were told, the producers were irreverent (perhaps even non-Canadian) in their production practices. I watched their news stories whenever time permitted.

An activity I found entertaining was to make reference to some story from the *Sun News* in the presence of any group of truly modern Canadian citizens (these folks are made obvious by their holier than thou attitude and their rose-coloured glasses). The mere mention of *Sun News* caused their eyes to roll toward the ceiling as they exchanged knowing glances to ensure themselves that they were all fully aware that they are, again, in the presence of another one of "those." It takes a rather rude slob like myself to enjoy such chain yanking; however, it was obvious that these folks had been trained or brainwashed to accept the politically correct screening of information made available to the Canadian taxpaying citizens by our two primary and heavily subsidized news sources.

The folks who were ready to point out the shortfalls of this non-Canadian news broadcast situation are also reluctant to look at any information that may indicate the ugly accuracy of it. Their minds are made up and they certainly do not need additional information to cloud their visions. The easiest course of action for these "true and believing Canadians" was to simply discount and disregard *Sun News*. Should any of these pure folks take a moment to watch some of those broadcasts, they would find themselves doubting and questioning a large part of the information they have been carefully programmed to accept as fact.

As I write these stories, I have learned that *Sun News* television programming has ceased operations due to lack of government funding and the limited advertising revenue they were able to generate. No doubt there was a reluctance among Canadian politicians to make any funds or support available to this organization because of their challenging habit of reporting all sorts of questionable actions by our government bureaucracies. In my limited knowledge of such things, I am convinced that our nation is a lesser place for all of us due to the folding of this news organization. There will, however, have been rejoicing among many who consider themselves loyal and educated Canadians.

The remaining television, radio, and print news media of our nation have completely overlooked the folding of *Sun News*. Obviously, such an incident is of little or no consequence to the politically correct and public mind-controlling media. They have simply heaved a great sigh of relief and kept quiet about it. Obviously, the Canadian population has been judged to be in no need of information or explanation about this closure. This is another disgusting reality of our acceptance of the detailed screening and politically correct reporting of news in this country. Neither of our heavily subsidized main broadcasting networks were able to find the time or inclination to make the public aware of this somewhat major event.

Sun News, on an early November evening in 2014, did an interview with the chief of a central Saskatchewan native band. The interview was like a breath of fresh air, in that the chief is a well-spoken man with a modern and progressive attitude about the future and presence of the native people in Canada. The interview was done in the open air near the chief's hometown. He was dressed in a business suit, as would be expected of a man who takes his conduct and leadership as a serious matter in the modern world. The wide expanse of the Saskatchewan skyline was clearly and beautifully displayed as the background for the interview. The chief was obviously proud to be the leader of a band of natives who have attained almost total employment in the booming Saskatchewan economy, and he told how they work together to ensure that this situation continues. They encourage education and training among their people to ensure that some of them will be ready and able to fill almost any employment opportunity that becomes available, not with a view of being the "token Indian" but rather by being the best qualified applicant for the job. They are obviously not concerned about the frequent complaint of lack of native educational facilities. Their young people are using the long-established facilities available to any Saskatchewan residents. There was no mention of the common native demands for land claims, treaty rights, cash handouts, or the blockading of some Canadian industrial project. It seemed obvious that this man and his people are not as concerned about such things as most of his fellow natives in other areas of Canada are.

Neither of the major Canadian television broadcasters found the opportunity to interview this man or the native leaders in some of the other progressive areas, such as the South Okanagan tribe in British Columbia, or some of the Blood Tribe of southwestern Alberta. Obviously, there is some discreet policy or program in place to deter major television producers from such an endeavor. The *Sun News* interview displayed a progressive and positive attitude among these Saskatchewan natives, wherein they are endeavoring to take an active part in the world they have all been born into.

Sadly, there appears to be some government or similar program in place to discourage the wide distribution of these positive actions by these modernized natives. Surely there would be many Canadian natives and Canadian citizens in general who would find such programming of great interest and beneficial to the natives in all other parts of the nation.

There is a strong possibility that this thought pattern or prevention program originates with the Federal Department of Indian Affairs and Northern Development. This huge government department obviously has a large understanding of their responsibilities to the natives of Canada; however, they have a greater respect for the continuance of the employment of every one of themselves and are fully aware that progressive actions among the natives, as in this Saskatchewan tribe, may be the beginning of the end of their careers.

There is little doubt that such an obvious situation in this long-standing government department could bring about programs that prevent or deter actions among the natives such as those referred to here. The care and nurturing of the natives of Canada has become almost an industry in the federal government, and the continuance of this industry depends on the dependence of the native people on the actions of this agency. Any good employee of this huge agency will see this problem and not encourage such actions by the Canadian natives. They will do whatever they can to avoid making such events common knowledge to the Canadian populations of natives and others where such actions do happen. There will, therefore, be little or no need for a firm, written policy to not distribute such information.

This is an example of one of the few effective programs to assist the Canadian natives having been planned and designed by the natives themselves. I suspect that the folks at the Federal Department of Indian Affairs and Northern Development are feeling a "chilling draft" from such actions among their previously loyal subjects.

Chapter 24
Misappropriated Funds

Another recent news story in the Vancouver Island papers told of government funds in the amount of $31 million getting into the hands of a group of natives who claimed they were planning to look after child welfare problems within their British Columbia communities. The funds are gone but the auditor could not find any evidence of a single child having benefited in any way. A day or two after that news release came the story of the Innu Development Limited Partnership in Labrador. Employees and managers in this organization were paid tremendous amounts in salary. One manager received $1.5 million (tax free) over a five-year period, while his close friend and assistant manager received $717,000 (tax free) during the same period. There is no obvious public record of what, if anything, was accomplished by the expenditure of huge amounts of government funds.

The newspapers frequently carry such stories. Among the most recent was the announcement on February 8, 2014, from an aboriginal gathering at Standoff, Alberta, that the federal government is prepared to deliver $1.9 billion over the next five years to get aboriginal education totally into the hands of the native executives and leaders. This money is said to be protected by a 4.5 percent adjustment clause to shield it from inflation. Tragically, the announcement made no mention of any other provisions to protect the money.

It seems obvious that the dismal track records of most native groups in dealing with hand-out money has little to do with the acceptance and financing of the next scheme. It appears that our politicians and bureaucrats are brain dead in such matters. The history of the misuse and abuse of handout money among the Canadian natives should certainly have generated some fear or caution in the doling out of more billions into this apparent sinkhole. Perhaps they are so frightened by the potential vote loss that they cannot bring themselves to ask some necessary questions and demand extensive audit processes to try to control the abundant abuse of handout funds. This is amazing when we consider the long list of financial disasters in the past and then look at the eager and willing politicians with our cash in their sweaty hands.

Among the most recent and never-ending reports of amazing financial corruption on native reserves is the story from the Shuswap Reserve with headquarters near Invermere, British Columbia. This story made the news about the end of October 2014. The Shuswap native band has another reserve in the North Okanagan on the shores of Shuswap Lake near Chase, British Columbia. The chief for both reserves is a very old man who shares leadership responsibilities with his former wife and a son from a former marriage. The Internet is full of grand stories of the progressive and ambitious programs this band has accomplished over recent years, ranging from golf courses to tourist facilities and more. A chartered accountant, in a recent audit, reported expenditures of federal money by the band listed as "other" in an amount in excess of $2.5 million over two years. The chief received a salary that has averaged in excess of $250,000 tax free every year for the past five years, an amount that would require an annual salary of about $400,000 if it was earned by a taxpaying citizen. This amount breaks down to about $3,000 per year in wages for the chief for each of his resident band members. The former wife of the chief is paid in excess of

$200,000 annually, also tax-free. The son receives a tax-free salary in excess of $500,000. These nepotistic executives are responsible for a native tribe of less than 300 people, with only eighty-seven living on the reserves.

Another report states that there has not been a meeting of the band members or their counsel for eight years. A refreshing bit of information from Invermere indicates that some of the band members are becoming angry about the conditions they live under while their executives wallow in exorbitant amounts of money. This is a step in the right direction, even though it should have happened many years ago. Obviously, the Department of Indian and Northern Affairs has been found to be somewhat short of being on top of this saga.

Another recent tragedy unfolded at the Makwa Reserve near Loon Lake, Saskatchewan. Two toddlers died in a house fire on the reserve and our news media did a thorough job of the usual one-sided reporting of this sad event. The Loon Lake volunteer firemen had long before advised the reserve chief and his abundant staff that they would no longer attend fires on the reserve with their limited equipment and resources. Loon Lake has a population of 390 people, while the reserve has 923 people. The Loon Lake volunteers had attended prior reserve fires with the minimal fire equipment they can afford and had billed the reserve management $3,380.89 for their services. The reserve management had chosen to not pay that bill in spite of their annual federal government fire-fighting allowance of $11,000. Obviously, the reserve management had found more important uses for this money.

The reserve had been provided with a fire truck some years before, but it was left sitting on the reserve until it was almost hidden in the brush that had grown up around it. The Makwa people have been unable to organize a

---

volunteer fire service among their population. Obviously, they had higher priorities. The reserve chief talked about the refusal of the Loon Lake volunteers to assist with our news people. The news report resulted in a number of articles on Facebook and other public media where the fire-fighting volunteers of Loon Lake were criticized severely for not assisting. The public seemed prepared to lay the entire fault on the non-native people who were near the scene of another native disaster. The chief and his six counsellors, including three with the same last name, are costing the reserve population nearly $1 million annually in salaries and expenses. All this money comes out of federal grants and allowances made available to this reserve and its leaders. The shame of this incident does not belong to the people of Loon Lake, but to the reserve where the chief and his nepotistic council spend more than $100,000 every year on cell phones.

Chapter 25
Preservation of Native Cultures

The emphasis on the idea of preserving native "culture" has done little or nothing to improve the lot of the average native person today. There should be some effort put to preserving their history and culture, but not to the exclusion of the harsh realities of the world we live in today. The foundations of the native cultures are gone; only memories can be maintained in the world today. There are no places left on the globe where a hunter-gatherer culture can survive. This is only one of the realities the natives and the rest of us must face. The original native culture in the world of today can only exist in dreams.

Another difficult aspect of the retention of the native culture is the obviously lesser concern in their culture for the value of life. In another chapter, I raised this lesser concern among the natives about the protection of life. They were prepared to live by the whims of nature and, therefore, had to be prepared to lose some of their loved ones when nature did not provide for them as they had hoped. The native culture accepted these tragedies and continued with little thought of ways and means to prevent such natural events in the future.

Our governments and all of us, as a misinformed society (about native affairs), make the lot of our natives worse through efforts that sustain and enforce the notion that the natives had a utopian existence until the arrival of the New

World explorers. These modern people suggest that the first Europeans, or whoever first landed in North America, should have simply packed themselves back onto their boats and sailed away because there were already human inhabitants here, even though some of them were living in holes in the ground. That concept might have a slim chance of prevailing in our modern world, with all our proper thinking folks making unrealistic decisions; however, we must keep in mind that the original explorers and traders were in a very different mindset during those early explorations. Hopefully, there are not many modern wishful thinkers who, with their rose-coloured glasses, could thoughtfully entertain that "sail away again" possibility for more than a few hours. The basic human drive to explore and conquer has been abundantly obvious in humankind since before the first recorded history.

Many of our ancestors looked at the vast oceans of the world as more than a source of food. They immediately thought of the possibility that there was something out there just beyond the range of sight. Once that thought had established itself in the minds of these people, they began to feel the need for boats and a method of propelling them. Over time, these ambitious people developed the ways and means to satisfy their driving curiosity. Obviously, this drive and ambition had not established itself on the shores of North America until these curious people began to arrive here.

Another undisputable fact of human history is the need to defend ourselves, our possessions, and our perhaps questionable claims to our accidentally chosen areas of the Earth. The natives of North America had no concept of land or property ownership. They were mostly nomadic people who drifted with nature's provisions. The only restriction on their movements came from a stronger or larger tribe who would probably kill intruders if the opportunity was presented. Rivers or mountain ranges served as approximate tribal boundaries, with occasional minor scrimmages or all-out primitive wars taking place along most of these arbitrary border locations. The strongest and most capable fighting tribe would vanquish their nearest rivals in a manner similar to the conduct of humanity around the globe. Today, the natives are laying land claims to nearly all of the country, not necessarily based on reality but because they are receiving a more than favourable reaction from our vote-hungry politicians, our wishfully proper-minded bureaucrats, and all our modern thinkers with their rose-coloured glasses.

In every case, the native claims are based on tribal areas that existed at the moment in history when our ancestors began to arrive in the Americas. The newcomers recorded the existence of these tribal areas and today their descendants are being held to the fire because they did that. There is no doubt that these tribal areas changed hands many times over the unrecorded centuries prior to the new arrivals, yet today we are asked to be totally responsible for the rights of those who held the land areas at the moment in time when our ancestors arrived and began making recorded history.

The future holds some alternatives. If the native land claims are all satisfied to meet the rising expectations of these people, this nation would revert to what it was before the first explorers laid eyes on it. The present population would have no means to provide for their basic needs and they would be forced to seek some alternative. This is a harsh position to put forward; however, it is not without real potential. Even the majority of our city dwelling population could find themselves facing this situation in the not too distant future.

The Great Wall of China was constructed out of necessity about 2,500 years ago. The people of North America, with few exceptions, were still in such a primitive situation that they were unable to organize themselves and present a defense against the arrival of the new people. While some research indicates there may have been human inhabitants in the Americas for a time equal to any other region of the Earth, they had not developed culturally or socially to the point where they could work together to present a defense against what obviously could have been (and was) the beginning of the end to their way of existence.

When the first foreigners arrived here, the natives of North America were struggling to develop better and more efficient ways to attack and destroy their neighbouring tribes, and similar activities are still prevalent among much of humanity today. Archaeologists have found abundant evidence of attacks and all-out wars among the numerous native tribes in North America, and many of these tribal battles are confirmed to have happened long before the arrival of the first offshore invaders. The natives of this part of the world are people like all the rest of us; they have no shortage of human frailties and weaknesses. Intertribal warfare and distrust was as much a part of their day-to-day existence as anywhere else on the globe. The strongest tribe in these battles took rewards in the form of slaves; young people not killed in the battles became slaves to the vanquishing tribe. The thought of, and the great need for, a defense against offshore invaders of their lands had not occurred to them up to that time, or perhaps they would have formed some strong tribal alliances for that purpose.

Today we are told of the vital need to preserve native cultures in spite of their obviously lesser respect for life in their culture. The development of a written language would have provided records for the natives to base their decisions on and they could perhaps have been much better prepared for and understanding of the possibility of foreign invasion. The annihilation of a number of North American tribes occurred long before the arrival of the first offshore invaders. This has been revealed by the work of archaeologists and others since the new people arrived. This fact raises questions about native conduct and deportment long before the arrival of the newcomers and the destruction of their allegedly flawless way of life.

Chapter 26
Control of the Public Mind

Public opinion and knowledge are influenced by people who have made a science of controlling this aspect of our existence. Politicians, the mass media, special interest groups, clergy, the police, and any group with an axe to grind have learned and refined the intricate art of influencing the mindset and attitude of the public at large. The attitude and thinking processes of even highly educated people have been influenced by these activities. A large part of this mind manipulation is accomplished through the careful screening and alteration of the information made available to the masses; political correctness plays a large part in this process.

Humanity in nearly every area of the world has learned through many wars that gathering intelligence information is vitally important to the outcome of every military action. Spying and espionage are a necessary part of national security. In addition to simply spying and seeking agents in other countries, modern warfare now includes groups of people whose entire purpose is to distribute disinformation for the purpose of creating doubt and a lack of cooperation among those parties who consider each other to be allies. This former military practice has now spread into nearly every aspect of our daily lives, where various special interest groups continuously manipulate the information that will be made available to the masses.

A balanced report by any of our mass media institutions, providing all the facts of an issue, is seldom provided. Partial information that embellishes or exaggerates some aspects of a situation is the rule, not the exception, with the goal being to support a chosen position while excluding contrary facts.

The information spread widely among our present population about the native way of life and their original existence is a shining example of this deliberate disinformation. A previous paragraph told of the oversight of a luxury vehicle abandoned on an isolated reserve. Who among these news people is responsible for the obviously willful failure to depict such an image to the Canadian taxpaying viewers? This person must be the holder of a master's degree in political correctness and mind control of the masses!

Many well-meaning people have grown up with this attitude and had it added to by others who, in most cases, have only textbook experience on which to base their beliefs. Many of these folks with their rose-coloured glasses are actually true believers in what they have been taught over their years of controlled research and learning. They truly believe that the truth is not something to be distributed willy-nilly to the Canadian taxpaying population. Information of this type will only serve to stir up resentment and embarrassing questions for the politicians and bureaucrats who have dutifully made funds available to these voting people. They are all very aware of the consequences of providing readily available but contrary truths, and they do not want any part of such things.

Chapter 27
Real Nature

Most mainstream Canadian people of today actually believe in the wonderfully kind and generous attributes of nature, and that a positive attitude will carry any one of us through life without experiencing failure or disappointment. These folks believe that the natives of all of America had a utopian existence in total harmony with nature and that Old Mother Nature looked after every detail of their life requirements.

In reality, many modern-day people have never experienced nature in the raw. They have read and been told of the miracles of nature but the harsh and often bitterly cruel aspects of nature have not been experienced by most because the majority of our modern population have grown up almost totally away from the brutal facts of nature. The greatest part of our modern population have been born and raised in large cities. They believe it is their duty to look only at positive aspects that support their beliefs and to disregard all possibilities and probabilities that may point to some other conclusions.

Having grown up in a rural setting on the Canadian prairies, I can see the benefit of some of these beliefs, but I also witnessed aspects of nature that brought strong and totally reasonable questions to my mind. These sights and experiences are outlined in an earlier paragraph, so I will spare the reader repetition of these hard facts of life. Ignoring the realities of nature will not bring about an existence closer to the way we wish things were or the way we would like them to be. It can only leave us in a worse situation, because we are making judgments and decisions without the life experiences necessary for such actions.

Over unrecorded history, the natives of the Cariboo region of British Columbia starved and froze to death in their wintering holes in the ground, not by any plot or plan, but by the actions of nature and the choice by the natives to not find more effective ways to cope with the realities of their existence. This, too, was nature in its full effect— "survival of the fittest." To their credit, the natives of those times were prepared to live with these tragedies and the results of obviously faulty choices by their leaders. The native people of those times possessed a different outlook than most of us have today, and to a large extent, the modern thought patterns and procedures were brought to this country by the early settlers and traders.

The native people have adopted some portions of this mindset, along with their need for the medical miracles available today. They cry out for medical aid, emergency services, fire protection, and whatever other services are available from the concerned and hard-working people who they will, in the next moment, be critical of, in the belief that their lives would have been far better if these people had not arrived on the scene.

Chapter 28
Modern Fixed Mind

There is a tendency to form strong opinions about issues that affect our day-to-day lives, and this tendency increases proportionally with the weight or public appeal of the issue. Once we have established an opinion and gathered what we see as a body of evidence to support our opinion, we tend to then disregard any facts or contentions that do not support our thoughts and accepted beliefs. We will accept and propagate only the points of information that, in our mind, make our case stronger. Any material or facts contrary to our beliefs and thoughts will be ignored and summarily discarded.

This somewhat illogical system has served humanity well in a variety of events over our history but it has also been a major contributing cause of mistrust, hate, and war. This very human tendency is abundantly obvious in the world of today in politics, advertising, religion, public relations, justice, and most other areas of human interaction. The result of this win-or-lose system often gives the benefit of a decision to the party that was better financed and best prepared to support their position by whatever methods and means are required to secure the win. Valid facts and contentions put forth by the opposing person or group of persons are shoved aside as though they were all evil lies, entirely without justification.

Our provincial and federal government systems are prime examples of this. The opposition must oppose every plan or submission put forth by the government of the day, not necessarily because of flaws or problems or weaknesses within the suggested action but only because they are the opposition.

Surely the time has arrived for humanity to put their best resources into the search for a system that will be better able to look at every aspect of every situation and make more use of compromise and cooperation. Such a system will have to look at every aspect of each situation and apply rational thought and analysis, without regard to possible embarrassment or discomfort (due to political correctness). I wish I could outline here just how this new thinking should be established, but I am able only to speculate at this time. It will require re-thinking many of our present ideologies and a dedicated effort by experts in the fields of inter-human relations. I do not fit well with that crowd.

There is little doubt that one of the first steps in this process in Canada will be a long and hard look at our infatuation with political correctness. The tragic situations of many of the natives and other minorities across Canada are complicated by our inability to discuss any issue that may cause embarrassment or bring questions to the positions taken by these people. The preceding paragraphs about recent native financial disasters are a clear example of this lack of anyone willing to question their financial blunders or, in most cases, just plain fraudulent conduct. There are many portions of these stories concerning the flagrantly bad behaviour by the leaders of many native bands across this country, but few of these events where the general population of natives raised concerns about the criminal or near-criminal behaviour by their chosen leaders. This odd behaviour leads one to think that the majority of the natives are prepared to accept graft and excessively high salaries for their leaders as though it was completely natural, and their leaders were entitled to do this. There is a possibility that some research into this aspect of native conduct would partially explain their confidence in their leaders. I believe this strange conduct is an established myth, supported by superstition or religious beliefs. When a leader has been appointed or selected, their culture does not allow for questions about this person's conduct.

Every discussion undertaken in negotiations with the natives is tainted by the imagined need on the Canadian government side to discuss only positive things about the native way of life and their actions and inactions before and since the arrival of the foreigners. There can be no denial that the natives across all the Americas were dealt a life altering blow and a loser's hand when the first explorers, traders, and settlers arrived. The term *loser's hand* applies more accurately if one goes along with the majority in their belief in the idealistic native way of life here before the foreign invasion.

There have been opportunities to help these people adapt their lives to the new reality and make the most of the unalterable situation they are born into. In most instances, where a good, solid proposal was put forward, the natives were suspicious of the action or they simply could not bring themselves to try to change or to adopt something new. Genuine and carefully planned opportunities are seldom made available because our infatuation with political correctness does not allow anyone to suggest that there were and still are some ways to improve on the original native way of life. We are led to believe that the natives of North America lived an idealistic life, where everything was grand and good.

This faulty thought pattern is perpetuated even in the face of indisputable evidence that many of these people lived in holes in the ground or in teepees during Canadian winters. These places were marginally heated by an open fire in the center of the structure, with the only fuel available to those on the open prairie being dried buffalo dung. There were no stovepipes or chimneys to take away the smoke from either the wood fires in the forested areas or the shit fires on the open prairie. The smoke from these marginal heat sources would not have been a pleasant or healthy thing.

This was the reality of life for those tough and hardy people in those times. There is little doubt that many of the native populations of today would not have the stamina or the will to endure such an existence, yet they are all fully convinced that their lives were positive and wonderful until the invaders took it all away from them. This is a hard fact that will have been dealt with by the traditional oral history among the natives. This is the sort of material from oral history that can be "taken to the bank."

Chapter 29
Harsh Realities

The buffalo and the salmon and most wild game animals are all but gone and they will never come back in the abundance that allowed primitive hunters to survive. This is the harsh reality these people are faced with, and there is a need to bring this ugly fact to the negotiation table even though it is not a comfortable and politically correct point of discussion. The natives of today must prepare themselves by having and listening to forthright discussions and by doing careful and accurate investigation about every aspect of their former and mainly imaginary ideal lifestyle. They must accept that a large portion of their former life was a grim and unrelenting struggle.

The natives of today should find some pride in this examination of their past because the residents of North America were cut from tough material or they would not have survived to witness the arrival of the newcomers. The basic needs of the imagined utopian life that the natives and many of the newcomers of today like to dream of are gone, and nothing will bring these things back. Their cultural dreams seem real to them and these things should be carefully and accurately preserved, within reason; however, we must all bear in mind that the daily requirements of life cannot be produced by chanting and beating drums.

Chapter 30
If the Old Days Came Back

If the great fairy godmother of our imaginations were to wave her magic wand and take all the natives of today back to their imagined idealistic way of life in the year 1400 or earlier, there would be a devastating die off in the first winter. This die off would occur even if the fairy godmother also brought back the buffalo and all the fish and game to the natural levels of that time period.

These people talk about their utopian existence before the arrival of the invaders, but a detailed and factual examination of their actual circumstances leaves little doubt that almost none of the present-day natives would have the strength and grim determination of their ancestors to tough it out as those hardy people did long ago. This impossible, imaginary transformation should also include the return of all the native methods available in those times and the elimination of all modern things, like firearms, cooking pots, motor vehicles, knives, matches, and insulated, centrally heated homes.

This hard set of facts would apply to many of us today. I would certainly not willingly spend a number of northern Alberta winters in the conditions my ancestors endured beginning in 1898. The original natives of Canada and all of North America were a tough, hardy, determined group of people. Without those characteristics, they would not have survived their primitive existence to see the first invasion of offshore traders and settlers. Their life was a tremendous struggle in the untamed wilderness of North America, a struggle that took many of them to what we would consider an early grave. Fate has not found a just reward for the descendants of those hardy people.

The natives of today have only a distorted understanding of the realities of their existence in the times before the invasion by traders and settlers from the Old World. The natives cannot be faulted for this clouding of their history. Fifteen or more generations have passed since any of these people lived in their original lifestyles. Any oral history that has been passed through all those generations will be distorted and willfully turned to appear as a totally positive thing. The native oral history we hear so much about can only add to this idealistic but incorrect recall of their non-history. The natives of today should do some deep research into the reasons there are far more of them in the present day than there were when the first non-natives began to appear on the shores.

Their total involvement with and their willful acceptance of the laws of nature had a great deal to do with this fact. Some valid research into the actual laws of nature that were and still are in effect will have a hugely enlightening effect, along with many other facts about their original existence. The present false information generously provided to the Canadian natives and all Canadian school students about the abundant provisions of nature will also require some thought, investigation, and correction.

Nature is wonderful in many ways; however, regular and consistent kindness and careful, considerate provision of the necessities of life are definitely not in nature's dictionary. Nature is a harsh master to those who choose not to take precautions against the very nature of nature.

Nature exists through the generous use of harsh methods. There is no thought process or due consideration in nature. If the weather pattern changes, then some creatures of nature will pay the extreme sacrifice unless they have taken action against nature by moving to a more survivable location or by learning how to store food during the times of natural plenty.

If we look closely at many of the original, ingenious inventions and discoveries by some early branches of humanity, we see that most inventions and actions by those early people around the world were to prevent the laws of nature from wiping them off the Earth. This is another of the ugly realities that must be dealt with by the natives and those who are involved in the provision of their present survival methods. The natives of North America lived or died by the laws of nature, the same natural laws that control the number of prey or predators at any time in the continuous cycles of nature.

Most of the policies and practices we have put in place during our history in North America have been of little actual benefit to the natives. These people have been left with a feeling of dependence and entitlement from well-intentioned policies and today most of them are no better equipped for the world as it is than they were at the time of the first arrival of offshore invaders.

Another fact to be considered is that there are far more people in Canada today who have native ancestors than there were at the time of the first invasion of traders and settlers. Those who fall into the loosely defined "native populations" of Canada are among the fastest growing segments of our entire population today. The natives in many locations in Canada have refused to cooperate with the Canadian census surveys; however, even the partial count available at this time clearly indicates that their numbers today are far in excess of the totals when the first explorers and traders arrived.

This fact raises more questions about the utopian life systems of the early inhabitants of Canada. An ideal or even a marginally efficient existence in those pre-explorer times should have left them with a much greater population. The germs and diseases that plagued Old World explorers had not reached the natives of the Americas. Their lesser numbers, therefore, must be accounted for by other causes, such as tribal warfare, starvation, and exposure.

Chapter 31
Alcohol and School

Among the early arrivals from the Old World were people who were totally motivated by greed and criminal conduct. Some of these greedy people were not long in discovering the aboriginal weakness for, and the almost total lack of control over, the consumption of alcohol. We Canadians like to tell anyone who will listen that all the evil whiskey traders came across the border from the United States. There is, however, an abundance of evidence to show that there were also a generous number of homegrown scoundrels involved in this lucrative activity.

The extreme thirst for and weakness against the effects of alcohol among the natives became evident in their first encounters with this substance and many lucrative business opportunities became abundantly obvious. The whiskey trade was devastating to the natives from coast to coast in North America, and is still a major problem to many of these people today. This weakness is still a major problem among these people, but it is not confined exclusively to Canadians of native origin. There are many of us among nearly all racial groups who cannot or will not control their use of alcohol, and the overall costs to our society are staggering.

The tragic inability to control the consumption of alcohol among the natives was clearly documented in Canadian history about 200 years before the first residential school experiment was attempted. The early settlers were in a position to observe many aspects of the original native lifestyle. These early people concluded that by making education available to the native youth, a gradual change would come about among these people; however, they could then clearly see that education required daily attendance by the native youth and this could not happen with the alcohol-induced mayhem among the natives.

In our modern, politically correct approach to all things, the natives have been taught and they are willing to believe that the alcohol intolerance among them is a direct result of the evil inflicted on them by the failed and faulty attempt at compulsory education in the residential schools. A more accurate assessment of the many reasons for the implementation of these schools involved the obvious native weakness for alcohol. A family unit involved in the abuse of alcohol cannot and will not be able to get their children organized and off to school or to any other daily activity.

The native weakness for the effects of alcohol became a major factor in their difficulties in dealing with the sudden loss of their natural way of life and it is still the most challenging thing that many of them face today. Our politically correct pretense that the situation is directly attributable to the failed schooling system can only make a bad situation worse. The ugly truth must be dealt with, but there is no easy way to accomplish this. Today, the rapidly growing aboriginal segment of the Canadian population is plagued by fetal alcohol syndrome, and the numbers continue to grow because there is no will or effort being put forward to clearly identify the problem and deal with it.

Both the modern mainstream politicians and most certainly the many well-paid native leaders consciously avoid the need to address this obscenity. Our pretending and support of the native hypothetical position that their alcohol intolerance is due to something as vague and unlikely as their residential school difficulties and alleged abuses of previous generations can only promote more alcohol dependence among these people and a lack of desire to even try to correct this damaging behaviour.

Chapter 32
Deliberate Spread of Disease

The majority of natives today have been taught and they are willing to believe that the foreigners came here with only malicious intentions for them. This theory is widespread in our society and is propagated by the current educational programs provided to Canadian students, who have been led to believe that evil toward the natives was, in fact, the sole intent of early arrivals. There were some situations that support beliefs along this line; the case of the Beothuk natives of Newfoundland is one, although I raise this issue reluctantly because it does not support my preconceived view of the entire situation.

There are two schools of thought about the Beothuk. One is that, because they were among the first North American natives to come into frequent contact with the foreigners, they were devastated by exposure to diseases they had no resistance to. The second is that the newcomers hunted and killed them into extinction. The hunting and killing theory seems to be the one favoured by our schools and scholars today, but there is certainly ample room to argue that diseases were the main cause of the demise of these people.

This brings up the long-standing story that the invaders deliberately brought smallpox and other contagious diseases to the natives on infected blankets or other trade goods. This dastardly deed was supposedly done at a time when human learning had not advanced beyond a vague understanding of infectious diseases, viruses, and germs. The Canadian schools perpetrate this deliberate disease theory to all modern-day students in spite of the obvious lack of creditability.

If we give this theory some analytical thought, we must question the suggestion that early explorers and traders risked exposing themselves to such a scourge, even if they did have some understanding of germs and contagious diseases. In spite of the obvious weaknesses in the deliberate disease conveyance theory, it is part of the teaching in our schools, particularly those of the native Canadians, as though it was an irrefutable fact.

The current example of our modern natives clearly displays how such a story would be spread far and wide. They are well schooled on the evils of the invaders. Perhaps they should give some thought to the attitude of the modern Canadian non-aboriginals who are so tolerant of the native mindset. Many of these folks are descendants of the original alleged evil bastards who first discovered North America and settled here. The human experience with communicable diseases since those times would indicate that diseases do not require a great deal of assistance to be distributed among mankind; however, these facts do not enter into the picture and they are apparently not welcome additions to the theories preferred by many ultra-modern Canadians. We are all asked to accept as fact that not a single person from the Old World boarded a ship while unknowingly carrying any of the many infectious diseases of those times.

There are strong doubts about this deliberate infection theory. One of the most valid difficulties with the truth of this theory is that all who took part in this alleged death-dealing plan would have to be aware and be prepared to kill most or all of the natives or to at least cause much suffering and pain among these people. For such an evil plan to have any chance of success, this number would have to include the majority of these early traders and settlers. We must be prepared, therefore, to accept and believe that most of these new people willingly participated in a group effort to exterminate the natives by whatever means were available.

Some analytical thinking will raise more doubt than belief in this evil theory. A large percentage of the early settlers would have to be aware of such a plan for it to have any chance of success. If such had been the mindset of the majority of the new people, then they could have quite simply found grounds to declare war on the natives and killed them. The deliberate disease transmission theory would have required a deep understanding of not only the conveyance of invisible and dangerous germs and viruses, but the knowledge and understanding of the natives' lack of immunity. This plan would also require acceptance and approval of the majority of the traders and settlers of efforts to exterminate the native people. If such an action had been the accepted goal and desire of the early traders and settlers, as we are now being educated to believe it was, then there would not be a native problem today.

Such savage actions and intentions among these early new people are hard to accept. If we can accept that these early new arrivals were capable of such diabolical actions, then we should also look at a far more obvious extermination method that was readily available to them without the risk of bringing diseases to themselves. The option of warfare is obvious; the arming and basic training of one side of a native tribal war would have been effective if their objective had been extermination. Any of the numerous inter-tribal hatreds could have been manipulated into a complete slaughter of one side or the other by simply providing firearms to one side. Had one side of any of these tribal wars been issued with firearms by these allegedly cruel and vicious settlers, the next battle would certainly have been the last for the tribe relying on the long established and marginally effective native weapons. The new people had total control of the supplies of ball and powder, so had little fear of the surviving natives turning the arms against them after the manipulated battle. With the lack of ball and powder, the natives of those times would immediately abandon the then-useless and heavy muskets, and the arms could be recovered for issue to the next conflict.

This evil plan would have been much simpler than the transmission of disease and much easier to accomplish, yet history makes no confirmed mention of such action in any of the many places where it could have been used. The early war between the Huron and Iroquois may have been one incident where such actions may have occurred. If we are to accept the deliberate transmission of diseases to the natives, along with the great risks of such actions, then the firearm theory, along with its most often non-happening, must also be explained by some of these modern thinkers among us. I do not envy the person assigned to this task. If they wish to support the theory of deliberate disease transmission, they have their work cut out for them.

The earliest arrivals from the Old World were mainly involved in the fur trade. Many of these men took native wives or promoted prostitution among the native women. Venereal disease flourished during those times and the native populations would have been completely infected in a short time. To date, the deliberate disease transmission theory has been directed toward smallpox and similar infections. There seems to be little desire among our native historical researchers to discuss the facts of venereal diseases. These infections were non-fatal in most instances and, therefore, do not support the evil plots that would have been required to bring the more deadly diseases to the natives. However, where the one type of disease was rampant, we are being trained to believe that a concerted effort was necessary to bring the other.

Perhaps perpetrators of the deliberate disease transmission theories could provide more detail to explain these differences. The sexual activities of the early traders among the native women resulted in considerable numbers of mixed-blood offspring, to the extent that the Riel Rebellion came about, where large numbers of these people struggled for a meagre existence that was aggravated by their being neither native nor immigrant. These wars were a large part of the reason for the establishment of the North West Mounted Police in 1873, and the struggles went on for more than a century. Some effort was put forth to have these "half-breed" or Metis people granted aboriginal status in some provinces; however, dominion-wide decisions were never made.

In the world of today, some natives from the many tribes across Canada have begun the difficult task of taking an active part in the world they were born into. There can be no valid argument put forth that the native populations of North America were not dealt a tremendous history-changing blow by the arrival of the explorers, an event they must yet overcome. Most certainly, there will be no going back, even though a great part of the modern native mindset is directed toward that impossibility.

Many of the native tribes actually welcomed the new arrivals with their new and advanced methods, knowledge, and trade goods. The tendency to welcome the newcomers came about largely because of the extremely primitive way of life that was prevalent and accepted among most North American tribes. Today, a large portion of the people involved in the many aspects of the native situation are trying to convince the Canadian majority of the wonderful lifestyles and living systems of the original natives. This false information is a tragedy and serves no useful purpose for either the native people or the modern Canadian citizens. It can only increase the hope among the natives that there will be a return to their former way of life where they all believe that life will be wonderful again.

Chapter 33
Winter Survival

Evidence of the extremely primitive living conditions that were considered normal by the natives was still visible in a number of locations around the central Cariboo region of British Columbia in the early 1970s, and may still be there today. These shallow impressions in the earth were the accepted way of survival among the natives as they endured the Cariboo winters. They lived in these shallow holes in the ground with only a temporary cover of a teepee to protect them from the frequent frigid weather conditions of northern British Columbia winters.

The shallow impressions, called kikwilly holes, were still clearly visible around Chimney Lake and Felker Lake to the west and south of the community of Williams Lake. The holes were dug out from the center and the removed earth was piled around the circumference to form a circular ridge. The holes were twelve to fifteen feet in diameter and are believed to have been covered by a temporary domed roof of tree limbs and animal hides or a teepee. The holes were only about half a meter deep near the center, where the fire pit was located. A small fire was maintained in the center of the hole and some of the smoke escaped through an opening in the center of the makeshift roof. The smoke hole would have allowed rain and snow to enter the shelter and heat to escape. Smoke from such an arrangement would certainly not find a direct escape outlet and the air conditions in these places must have been truly unhealthy for all the people, but especially for the elderly and infants.

Anyone who has lived through a number of winters in the central and northern Cariboo region is well aware of the extreme difficulties and near impossibilities of survival under such primitive conditions. Only the strongest among these natives could have survived in their chosen holes in the ground; the very young, the infirm, and the old would certainly have died a slow and difficult death. In spite of the severe hardship and the obvious tragic results of this living arrangement, these natives returned to the same holes in the frozen ground for the next winter and obviously they continued to do this year after year for centuries. Superstition and spiritual beliefs among the natives may have contributed to their reluctance or inability to develop or even to experiment with other living accommodations that may have brought about a better winter survival rate.

Obviously, the native people of those times were satisfied with their primitive existence and they were prepared to accept the annual loss of some of their loved ones due to these harsh and primitive living arrangements. A log structure with a stone fireplace and a woodpile could have improved their ability to survive the Cariboo winters. These simple structures could easily have been accomplished with the available Stone Age tools and resources, along with a considerable amount of hard work. However, centuries went by without any indication of an attempt at improving their winter living quarters. There are no places in the Cariboo where these kikwilly holes are still obvious that the natives have cried out to have a park established or a shrine erected. It would seem there is a lack of interest in preserving this aspect of their former existence.

No doubt there was a necessity for numerous burial sites around these kikwilly locations, yet there has been little effort to protect these graves from modern development. There have been such actions in many other locations, where industries or individuals have, perhaps unknowingly, encroached on ancient native burial sites. There seems to be varying degrees of concern from these people about their burial sites. In many cases, the background cause for these varying concerns would seem to be money.

Chapter 34
Lack of Resistance

Had the natives of North America been sufficiently organized and cooperative among their many tribes to present a unified resistance to the new arrivals, the history of those times may have been quite different. A realistic look at the scattered fragments of oral history available about their existence across the country indicates there was far more intertribal warfare, taking of slaves, and competition for territory than cooperation among the many tribes. We must acknowledge that this tragic history is not unique to the natives of North America. The early history of humanity in every area of the globe repeats and clearly demonstrates this weakness of the human psyche.

The new people, or invaders, whichever one chooses to call them, had advanced in the Old World to the point where they were fighting their wars and killing each other with cannons and muskets, while the North American natives were still fighting their wars with spears and arrows. This situation in America led to the limited or non-existent display of resistance to what obviously should have been understood as the beginning of the end of their allegedly cherished way of life. Perhaps the leaders of many of the tribal areas of this country could clearly see that a war against the invaders could have only one tragic result for them.

The history of mankind around the world is filled with stories of military action by one group to prevent a takeover by another, yet these people were unable to offer more than token resistance in a few scattered areas. Today, in our infatuation with political correctness, the descendants of the original settlers and all who have arrived since those times are considered totally responsible and financially liable for the tragic plight of the Canadian natives. This heavy burden of responsibility seems to be based on the actions of our ancestors or forefathers, yet the majority of the natives are unable and unwilling to even discuss the possibility that inaction by their forefathers and their chosen leaders during those early times was also a major contributor to the collapse of their way of life. This is another of the difficult facts that must be discussed to reach a more suitable situation for the modern-day natives of this country.

If our nation continues with the current blind acceptance of all responsibility for the native situation today, we should also give consideration to the picture our descendants will face in another 300 years. This suggestion should be given more consideration when we see the obvious reluctance in our present leadership and bureaucracies to give publicity and credit to the brave actions by some native tribes who have taken it upon themselves to move into and participate in the world they have all been born into.

There must be some policy or plan in place to prevent the spread of information and news about such significant events taking place among some progressive-minded native groups. How or why this is happening is a question that should be dealt with immediately. This is a question that will cause some discomfort among the many people who make their living from the "native industry." This question is perhaps a positive thing, as so many of the points raised here are directed at the actions or inactions of the natives alone.

Chapter 35
Limitations of Actions

Over the millennia of humanity on Earth, many laws and statutes have been drafted, adopted, and amended with a view to making life for the majority more fair and enjoyable. Statutes of limitations are among these. The first recorded laws about time and responsibility in connection to both civil and criminal actions date to the Roman times. Humanity around the world has retained these laws and guidelines since then. The basic function of these statutes is to establish a time limit beyond which a prosecution or appeal of a civil agreement or criminal action could no longer be pursued. The timeframes vary widely, ranging from five to twenty-five years.

No time limits have been assigned to the prosecution of some crimes, such as child abuse and homicide. The civil and contractual aspects of laws have been addressed with statutes of limitations in many countries. Today, effort is being put forth to acknowledge equality among all people of this Earth, yet we are still dealing with contracts and agreements that were drafted and agreed on hundreds of years ago. There is no doubt about the response from our modern, all-knowing justice system were some non-aboriginal Canadian citizen to pursue an appeal or an alteration of a civil action dated hundreds of years ago.

This is a touchy topic. If the actual time is given consideration, then the question must be asked: why did these people not do something about the many transgressions and delays in a somewhat more rational timeframe? We are asked to overlook this inaction by both sides of this thing and to simply accept the fact that the natives were not ready to deal with it during the first 300 years. The new Canadians who have been involved all these years are now being looked on as though they are totally responsible for this terrible delay. The facts must be carefully examined with a view to possibly assuming that some portion of this procrastination also belongs to the natives.

Chapter 36
Duties of Tribal Leaders

Almost every day of the year there are stories in the press about the plight and neglect of our native citizens. A recent one was about a tribe or clan in eastern Canada who, several centuries ago, was awarded an annual cash payment of four dollars for every native person living on that reserve. This agreement was approved in the range of 300 years ago and it has been ongoing since inception. The world was shocked to learn that this dollar amount had not been altered in all that time and, no doubt, many modern Canadian citizens feel shame at this.

The people involved in arranging the payment of this annual stipend should obviously have brought the lack of adjustment over the centuries to the appropriate government agency; however, some of us may not see this action as exclusively a part of their "evil white man" responsibility. Where were the well-paid leaders of the tribe? The suggestion that these leaders are responsible for this is closer to the fact than the modern trend to blame every such situation on modern government employees. The federal bureaucrats who have watched this thing for generations must have been aware of what was going on; however, the absurdity of it will have become an annual joke, and people who work in such surroundings certainly need something to bring them some gaiety, even though it happened only once a year. From their viewpoint, the logic of the entire thing could be summed up in an old prairie farm expression: "If it ain't broke, don't fix it."

A recent story in *The Victoria Times Colonist* was about the struggles with racism in our health system and the many aspects involved, from daily contact with the native people to the lack of specialized areas in our modern hospitals. The story tells of an unfortunate native woman on medication for the treatment of some medical problem that causes seizures. She tells of an ambulance attending her home when she was experiencing a seizure and that she overheard comments by one or more of the ambulance attendants to the effect that this was just another case of a drunken native abusing the ambulance system. This patient was hurt by these unthinking remarks and she tells in detail how wrong such an attitude is.

An aboriginal nurse also tells of her many experiences with similar attitudes among the medical staff in British Columbia. There is no doubt that such events are detrimental to the native patients, and action should be taken to further educate the medical emergency staff to avoid such outbursts during their duty.

The fault is directed totally to the modern workers and service providers of our vast medical systems, but these people are only human. Another aspect of such problems could be seen if some of these sympathetic people were to ride along with the emergency medical crews as they attend to the frequent calls for assistance from the native communities.

The keeping of statistics about the root causes of many of these calls for assistance would be politically incorrect in our modern and proper-thinking world. Alcohol and the uncontrolled abuse of it plays a part in far too many of these calls for service, and the assumption of another such incident is likely right from the opening of the door. This is a situation that seems to lack any positive action from among the natives. They demand improvement but do not see any reason for change to begin among themselves.

As a policeman working among our native people for many years, my memories of frequent emergency calls for assistance are abundant. There were, I am sure, some of these calls that were not the direct or indirect result of substance abuse, but I am unable to recall any at this moment. There is a short jump to an incorrect conclusion among emergency medical workers and the police; however, I hope some concerned citizens will give thought about why such things can and do occur.

The sad situation and the verbal outburst about the most likely cause of this incident are, indeed, unfortunate; however, the emergency responders stayed with the task at hand and saw to the evacuation of this person to medical facilities where she could be treated and properly cared for. This could have turned into a tragedy if the emergency responders had acted on their incorrect preliminary observations and just walked away. Such a situation would have certainly resulted in cries of racial discrimination. A recent statement about this has been circulated among many citizens: "Conduct has far more to do with racism than does skin colour."

Chapter 37
Non-Existent Words

In recent times, some deep thinkers have introduced non-existent words into the English language. These new words are not in keeping with the rules and proper use of English but they are in common use today in the mistaken belief that they will make the natives among us feel more comfortable or welcome. The native leaders should have protested vigorously to the introduction of words and spellings that have no place in their language and can only create a false image of the actual situation in their original culture.

A large part of the population today work diligently to convince us that the native ways were beyond reproach, and here we have an example of false information that seems to be intended to make the original life systems seem far more advanced than they were. The purpose of this altered language could be assumed to be aimed at convincing the world that the Canadian natives had an advanced method of reading and writing when, in fact, they used only primitive signs and markings to communicate among themselves in limited ways.

Here is a fabrication by some people who seem to believe that the more incorrect material that is made available, the better things will be for the Canadian natives. The hard facts are that, once again, we are creating disinformation, which in the long run can only make their situation worse. We are led to believe that the original native ways should only be looked on as great and wonderfully efficient methods in every way.

This presents another conundrum. The natives should be insulted by this attempt to bastardize their original communication methods and to create an inaccurate impression of their former allegedly flawless living systems. Many words from English have been applied to the original native way of life to create a false impression of their actual circumstances. The word *nation* is being applied to many of the loosely organized tribal clans from all over Canada. Until this change was quietly pushed forward, the word *nation* referred exclusively to societies with organized government systems, borders, military establishments, police, and an abundance of man-made plans and actions to maintain a livable society.

With the application of the word *nation* among the aboriginal people, we are being coerced to believe in a complicated society with involved government processes for all aspects of their existence and, most importantly, to deal with borders and territories and defense. The more common meaning of the word *nation* in our Western world includes the practice of almost open immigration. The native establishments in Canada are quite opposed to immigration; however, this does not seem to affect the use of that descriptive word. With this in mind, perhaps a great deal more background and history should have been applied to the establishment of native territories when the first written history was created by the new arrivals.

We are asked to accept native territories and demands for compensation based only on the history that was created by our early ancestors entirely, because there was no recorded history in the native way of life. The missing link in these records is the history of each of the native tribal areas. The question that has never been dealt with in regard to the existing tribal areas is this: how long had the then-current occupiers of these territories been there at the time of the arrival of the new people? These long-standing demands for territorial rights may be based on weeks of occupation or thousands of years. *First Nations* is another term in common use today to describe the variety of clans and tribes across the country. This wordplay adds to the hopes and expectations of the natives of today and goes a long way toward the expectation of their entitlement to everlasting compensation.

A variation of this wordplay is another large move in the replacement of the English words *whore* and *prostitute* with the phrase *sex worker*. This action by some of the deep thinkers in our modern society can only be looked upon as a step toward bringing some respect and perhaps even admiration to the oldest profession in this world. This replacement phrase, along with many others, defies all logic. We all know the meaning of the word *sex*; however, the term *worker* is a word that does not deserve to be used in such a manner.

There are many valid arguments in modern society about the terms *whore* and *prostitute* referring to only the female side of this human failure. It would seem that an opposite action would perhaps have been better suited to dealing with this wordplay. Some new phrases to bring more understanding and embellishment to the words *whoring* and *whoremonger* in reference to the male side of this trade would perhaps have served us better. The glorification of either side of this old trade is a questionable endeavor. The majority of the older generation, along with many of the present population, find it difficult to accept these new flowery terms, regardless of the illogical twist applied in the current requirement to satisfy an imaginary need.

A recent news story in the print media was about a young aboriginal mother who is taking steps to force the Vital Statistics Department of the North West Territories to accept non-English words and spelling symbols from outside our long-established Roman alphabet to supposedly produce some sounds from her native language. This young mother is attempting to force the territorial government to use non-English words in their records of vital statistics. Canadian governments have used only English and French in their recordkeeping over the entire history of Canada; we are now being pushed to introduce sounds and meanings from a non-written language. Her contention is that these sounds and symbols are a necessary part of her native language and are required to produce the sounds she wishes to apply to the naming of her infant daughter. It appears that this young mother is determined to have her way. This woman should be asked when or where the non-Roman spelling and symbols were found in the history and long traditions of her people.

Perhaps there are some lessons for us in this information from this young mother. Some of us may find it difficult to believe that her native tradition of non-written history held to the knowledge of a writing system that has never been in common use in the New World. It would seem obvious that the requested spelling symbols required for this traditional native name have little or nothing to do with the heredity and non-recorded history of the ancestors of this child.

Our society reaps the costs of our politically correct conduct and our overly generous attitude about granting almost any sort of alterations the natives can think of. The results of these actions over the past many years become more obvious as each request for special consideration from the natives becomes visible and audible. The young mother cannot be faulted for this request; she has probably been amazed by the success of past such demands from her counterparts.

These thoughts should be applied to the many "new" words being pushed into our language in our imaginary and urgent need to accommodate the desires of the natives and to rub our noses in the mainly imaginary evils done to the natives by our ancestors and all of us up to now. The imaginary ways of spelling many native words, such as the names of nearly every tribe in Canada, are used in news reports and other printed information. These new words appear to be some person's idea of how to spell foreign words that were never written or printed in the non-literate existence of the people they are trying to placate. If there had been ways of recording the pronunciation of any of these words, we, among the original natives, are still left with the passage of 300 or 400 years of oral history to base these new words on today—an impossible feat!

Chapter 38
Very Difficult Breakaway

With an upbringing on the Alberta prairie and many years of police work in the British Columbia interior, I have been in close contact with many native and part-native people. To this day, I think of some of these people as my friends and as people I would enjoy an opportunity to visit with again.

Many of these friends had long since left the native reserves and found their places in the world they were born into. These people were a strange mixture of thoughts and emotions; they were the first to utter a phrase that I frequently use in my writing: "Take part in the world you are born into." They had not totally abandoned their long-standing way of life, but were realistic enough to not dwell entirely on the impossibility of it ever being available again, for them or anyone else.

There are also some whom I count in this group of friends who still live within the confines of the reserve system. The strength and determination required by a native family to break away from the reserve can only be imagined by those of us who have not been through such a life-altering experience. This huge step into the realities of the modern world is made more difficult by misinformed people who spread false information about the native former existence and their inherent rights to nearly all of this nation. The individual native or native family who choose to break away from the dependence of their reserve lifestyle will be ostracized by those who are unable to find the strength to do likewise. This course of action does not show any abundance or lack of strength or weakness in the native people; it is simply a fact of human nature. These industrious and caring people will be labeled *apples* (red on the outside but white inside) by those who linger in the pride-sucking reserve life.

The present trends of pretending and wishing about the noble existence of the natives and, therefore, their rights to most of the territories of Canada are still in their infancy. Nearly every day there are more reports of the gradual but steady progress of giving our country back to the distant descendants of those who were squatters on some poorly defined and unmapped areas of this country at the time of the arrival of the first settlers and traders.

The natives of today have learned to take full advantage of our pliable justice system that is weighted to favour the imagined underdog. The natives hire expensive lawyers (using federal funds) and make more and more claims to this land. Our expensive justice system is prepared to listen to and believe a variety of information from those who base their claims on oral history. Our justice system will at the same time demand that any information presented on behalf of our modern society to be exact and backed by documentation and whatever else can be demanded of those who dare question the native demands, even in the half-hearted ways our system allows.

The need for special treatment of these primitive people at the time of their first encounters with our justice system is obvious; however; the assumed accuracy and validity of many modern native claims should be examined more extensively. The innumerable instances of gross mismanagement and corruption within the native communities should be food for thought when courts look at granting land claims and titles to the natives. With the track records of the natives, this land grab can only lead to a massive failure and the eventual end of Canada as it has become known. The native portion of the Canadian population will no doubt feel that such a complete failure of this nation would be a great accomplishment for them. If, however, they were to look into their current situation, they may realize that their entire existence has become reliant on the taxpaying citizens of Canada. The harsh fact is that their original and marginal way of life will not return automatically with the failure of this modern nation.

An interesting action took place in Alaska in 1972, when native land claims were extensively and expensively investigated and allegedly dealt with. The natives of that region were to become owner-occupiers of approximately 44 million acres of the state along with federal and state payments of $963 million. Keep in mind that those were 1972 dollars. The agreement was negotiated to contain a clause that would extinguish native land claims on other vast portions of the state.

At a glance, this seems to be a vast area and a huge amount of money, but to this date, none of the terms of that agreement have been dealt with on a permanent basis. This action was published as an example of the progress made on behalf of the Alaskan natives and no doubt caused some optimism among natives across North America and fear among those of us who will be affected by such actions. Forty-three years have passed since that announcement, yet the entire situation exists only in draft form in the hands of the natives and state and federal officials. This may be the record for procrastination by the justice systems and governments of the United States, Canada, and the native tribes of the area. The extremely expensive justice systems of the nations have developed the art of delay as their greatest contribution to our modern countries. The natives of all of North America have never had a strong desire for expedience; time has much less weight in their collective minds. This situation stands out as another example of the impossibility of a final settlement for the natives.

The justice system is not the only party responsible for this travesty. The natives must accept a large part of the responsibility for this lack of closure. Some material on the subject tells of a feeling among many of the affected natives that they could not bring themselves to agree to the extinguishment of their hunting and fishing rights outside the 44 million Alaskan acres that was to be deeded to them.

This is another clear example of the impossible path the natives are being convinced to follow. It seems clear that the problems of the North American natives will be dealt with by procrastination on both sides of the issue for at least another 300 years. This ugly fact adds to my contention that the natives should, individually, look long and hard at the difficult decision to adapt to the world they are all born into today. This huge step by each native would leave them with independence, freedom, and a feeling of pride of accomplishment. These things cannot and will not come about through the treaty and reserve systems.

Chapter 39
Leaving the Reserve

Growing up on an Alberta farm, my experiences left me with a belief that each of us has a responsibility for our own welfare and, to a lesser extent, for all those around us. With this in my background, I am almost totally at a loss to understand what forces are in place to cause so many native people to remain in the life-marginalizing reserve system. Anyone who has visited a reserve or even driven past one must have been impressed by the truly awful conditions prevalent on almost every such place in Canada.

Sadly, one of the most common reasons for this tragic behaviour is the never-ending promise of great wealth for all these people through the imaginary settlement of age-old treaties. The Alaska treaty settlement attempt is a clear example of the all but impossible goals in every similar situation across North America; that agreement was drafted in 1972 but it has not been signed into reality yet. Unemployment numbers in these places are beyond statistical data (prevented to some extent by political correctness); however, with nothing but time on their hands, there is in almost every case an obvious lack of any attempt to do simple home maintenance to keep up the appearance, condition, and comfort of their provided homes, or the grounds around them.

Obviously, many of these people are unable to visualize themselves in a living situation away from the reserve, but that difficult yet vital step is the only course of action available to achieve some semblance of a normal life in Canada today. The imagined wonders of their continued right to hunt and fish are truly mind-boggling. The hunter-gatherer days are gone, not only from this country but from our entire globe. No outcry for past rights or access, even if successful, will alter this fact. Obviously, many of these people are totally unhappy with their lot in life, yet there seems to be a limited number willing and able to make the vital decisions to do the necessary hard work to change their situation.

The people faced with the decisions regarding the continued existence of the native lifestyles found themselves with difficult questions. The native reserve system raised difficult points for the decision-makers of those times; they were faced with a rising population of newcomers and a lack of input or suggestions from the natives. The Indian reserve system was undoubtedly viewed as a temporary measure; none of the decision-makers of those times could possibly have thought that people would remain in such a situation for longer than it took them to gather themselves as families or individually and establish their own positive existence within the new society.

The newcomers to Canada were able to find employment or ways to earn their living, but the natives were unable to do anything similar for themselves. There is no doubt that there was reluctance among the new Canadians in regard to hiring natives, but there were many opportunities for anyone who felt the need for self-sufficiency in the rapidly advancing economy of those early times.

The demands for native self-determination are scary when one considers the track records of the aboriginals wherever they have been put in charge of financial management of the many projects attempted in the past hundred years. Mismanagement and incompetence in combination with fraud and theft seems to be the rule in the majority of such experiments, and the majority of the native people have just let it happen as though it was the proper and expected result.

The natives are in a tragic situation; that is certainly not from their conduct alone. They were overrun by other humanity in the same way as thousands or millions of others on this globe before them. This harsh fact leaves them with a difficult and limited choice; they can enter the modern world or remain in the marginalized reserve system as they have for the past several hundred years. These people were never on the gravy train we are told of. Life was far more difficult for most of them before the traders and settlers came on the scene.

Tragically, the combined efforts of both the natives and the newcomers have not found the answers. The modern trend by the natives and many newcomers is to only glorify the imagined wonders of life in America before the foreigners arrived. Political correctness overrules common sense and allows only for this one-sided investigation of the whole situation.

Chapter 40
Skills and Abilities

The story of Sacajawea, the young native woman who guided the Lewis and Clark expedition from the Dakotas to the Oregon coast and back, is a testimonial to the welcoming attitude on the part of many natives during those early times. The Lewis and Clark expedition was accomplished from 1810 to 1812, and may not have succeeded without the skilled assistance of this native woman.

Sacajawea was a Shoshone Indian by birth, but she had been captured as a child by the Minitaree tribe during a tribal war, and she lived as a slave until she was sold, as a young adult, to a French-Canadian trader, and she became his slave wife. The early life of this child does not support the modern tendency to glorify the idealistic way of life of the natives of North America before the foreign invasion. On the contrary, it is a glimpse into the harsh realities of their existence even though it is the tragic story of only one child of those times. A fact that seems worthy of some thought is that this child abuse occurred before the arrival of the evil invaders. This little girl was torn away from her family and tribe to become a slave to the enemy. If ever there were a valid cause for post-traumatic stress disorder, this would be a leading example.

In spite of her tragic experiences as a child, Sacajawea was a great benefit to Lewis and Clark, and their records are filled with admirable reports about her skill and abilities as a guide, interpreter, and negotiator on their behalf during their expeditions. There is some speculation that Sacajawea had another positive effect on the Lewis and Clark expeditions, simply by her presence. The natives who encountered the expedition would have been confused by the presence of a woman among the exploration party. Native war parties had always excluded women, according to the oral history of the many tribes and the records of the early arrivals. The fact that there was a woman in the Lewis and Clarke entourage would have helped convince the native tribes encountered along their route that this could not be a war party.

We should give some thought to the conduct and intentions of the French-Canadian trader who purchased this woman out of native slavery only to make her a slave to himself. She died giving birth to her second child near the end of the expedition. Her two children were taken into the homes of Lewis and Clark's families, where they were nurtured and raised to adulthood. This is another indication of the respect the two explorers had for this woman. There were no further references to the Canadian father of these children in the historical records that I was able to find. All indications are that when he became a widower, he simply abandoned his children to continue his wanderlust existence.

Chapter 41
Residential School Success

A story in one of my previous books was about a young girl who was taken away from her British Columbia home reserve and placed in one of the residential schools just as she reached school age. This young girl quickly demonstrated that she was a willing and capable student and she excelled in every aspect of the educational material presented to her. Contrary to all the information about these schools, this child excelled in the residential school system and continued there with help from some of the school and church staff until she had completed her high school education.

It seems obvious that this student managed to escape the continuous battery and other criminal offences said to be perpetrated on the students by the staff of these schools, according to the sworn testimony of the many native witnesses who testified before the Truth Commission hearings. The school staff were aware of this girl's abilities and attitude and they encouraged her to move on to a career as a registered nurse. She accepted their counselling and completed the three years of practicum and study with some help and encouragement from the staff at her former residential school, and she became a fully qualified Canadian registered nurse.

This intelligent young person received little or no encouragement or assistance from her home and family, yet she managed to excel at her chosen career. She had been working as a graduate nurse for a short time in a large eastern Canadian hospital when she chose to return to her birthplace for a short visit with her family and childhood friends over Christmas. The second day of her visit on her home reserve, a drunken potlatch broke out as a part of their routine Christmas celebration. Every adult resident of the reserve and many minors were intoxicated. A number of the young men who lived there became drunkenly amorous over this stranger in their midst and became abusive and threatening toward her. This frightened the young nurse so badly that she ran away into the winter night to escape their threats.

Her immediate family offered no assistance to this young lady, which raises another aspect of this tragedy; there may have been issues of prejudice. She was dressed in clothing suitable only for short walks on winter city streets. She froze to death on a low mountain pass she tried to cross to escape gang rape or worse. Her family should certainly have been aware of this situation, but they obviously did not care, or perhaps alcohol had eliminated their ability to think; or they simply could not be bothered to help her.

All attempts at the investigation of this horrible situation were stonewalled on the reserve. Her family confirmed the story but flatly refused to involve any of the perpetrators. Inquiries with other residents brought only general statements that confirmed the event as it is outlined here, but all those interviewed were careful to not provide any confirmable details.

There is little room to argue that the entire population of the reserve had not contributed in some way to the death of this capable young person. The advanced drunken condition of everyone at this tragedy was a main factor in the horrible outcome. Without the age-old custom and tradition of the drunken potlatch, this may not have happened.

Chapter 42
Failing Justice System

Today, the natives of many parts of Canada are vocal and organized in their complaints about the dominant society that they portray as being responsible for their current situation. These people, after many generations, are no longer strangers to the ways of the dominant society. If they choose to use the Canadian courts to further their objectives, then they should also be prepared to face a well conducted and valid defense. Their "no fault" attitude is reinforced by the majority of Canadians, who have sympathy for the natives but almost no first-hand knowledge of the facts and realities of their problems and, most importantly, the overall attitude among the majority of the native people themselves. Those in managerial positions, and many others in the justice system, are sympathetic and prepared to bend their decisions in favour of the natives in both criminal and aboriginal rights hearings.

This book is intended to shed some light on the realities of this situation. No doubt there are valid arguments to counter some aspects of this story; however, there are many more points raised here that leave little room for further questions. This situation is exacerbated by our educational material, which goes to great lengths to present a picture of the imaginary utopian existence lived by the natives before the invasion of the foreigners.

I, too, have sympathy for many of the natives I have come to know during my years of police service and as a child and young adult growing up near a large native reserve. Many natives I have come to know and respect do not need or want sympathy. They have chosen to live with and deal with the circumstances they were born into and they are doing as well financially and culturally as many of the rest of us, with the exception of them being ostracized by the "stay behind" remainders of their tribal clans.

The majority of the natives in this country, along with their ancestors, have existed over the recent centuries without contributing in any significant way to this process. The feeling of entitlement among these people provides the basis for inactivity and non-contribution to any aspect of their existence. The current policies and practices of our governments and government departments encourage no effort to assist natives to make this giant step into the modern world, most likely because such a program would be extremely politically incorrect and contrary to the predominant attitude of today.

The abundance of material about the original way of life among these people is slanted and embellished to present a picture of an almost ideal way of life among the natives before our ancestors came on the scene. I hope some of this material will cause some of our modern people to have another look, or at least try to get a better understanding of the harsh realities set out here. Today, these people seem determined to only promote plans and methods that will keep most of the native population in the unworkable and unacceptable situation they have experienced since colonization and before.

The attitude and conduct of the natives also contributes to the continuation of the unworkable living arrangements they constantly complain about. The well-being of natives who break with tradition and take part in the modern world is often more challenging, as they are ostracized by their kin and clansmen. Those who take this giant step into the unfamiliar reality of today should be looked on as a great example to the others, and they should be given assistance wherever possible for their display of courage, strength, and ambition. These few people have accepted the way things are today and have decided to deal with it. The current system tends to disregard these people and to immediately cut them off from the benefits available to those who remain in the unworkable and dispiriting native reserve system.

The assistance to and financial support for the Canadian aboriginals has become almost an industry in this country and it is certainly a large department of the federal government. We must look at the possibility that those in civil service and other areas of the native industry are more than a little unwilling to see the end of their employment through the integration and independence of the aboriginals. The obvious lack of support for the few native Canadians who attempt integration must be considered when dealing with this question. Is there any genuine interest from anyone in our large native industry to promote these positive and progressive actions by a few brave native Canadians?

An outstanding example is the previous mention of the natives in Saskatchewan, who have made such a positive move into the modern world but are not being given any encouragement or assistance with this huge undertaking. The lack of support extends even to the two major Canadian television operators, who have found no reason to support or encourage these brave people.

Chapter 43
Gradual Change

The native people of North America have been expected to change in a few generations the cultural and lifestyle patterns that came about over thousands of years in their wilderness home. Many in Canada have come a long way with these changes in a short time, historically speaking. Tragically, there are still many who must make those difficult changes, but to now, there have been few programs from within or outside the native communities that have shown any worthwhile progress.

The few programs undertaken within the native societies have a much greater success rate than any others. The success of these programs is understandable if we take time to realize that the natives will obviously be the experts in such developments. They have the complete understanding, and they know how to gain the support and respect among themselves to make such things functional.

I wish there was someone in our Department of Indian and Northern Affairs who could plan and outline a workable short-term solution to this monstrous situation, but nothing from there has been more than a stop-gap solution to date. The experiments by various levels of government have been expensive yet have a dismal record and have clearly shown that every effort to date has been far from the correct course of action. If there is a solution from outside the native populations of Canada, it has not been found in the past 300 years in spite of the continuous and obvious need.

Charles Scheideman

The infatuation among both the natives and the majority of Canadians with preserving the native culture can only be nonproductive. Many aspects of the native culture can and should be preserved among these people, but only to an achievable and functional level. The commitment to preserving a way of life that is no longer possible in the world today must be investigated and sorted out to achieve a balance between their lifestyle and culture and the hard realities we all must live with today.

The Canadian population today is a mixture of people from about every possible location and cultural background around our globe. All of these people are aware of their cultural history and background; however, few dwell on their past to the extent that they are unwilling or unable to deal with the realities of their daily lives. Contrary to such actions, many of these new Canadians are hard-working and dedicated to improving their lot in life while remaining aware of their cultures and traditions.

Chapter 44
Beginnings of Hope

There is a positive story from the South Okanagan area of British Columbia where a native chief has led a carefully selected group from his small tribe in a concerted effort to take an active part in the day-to-day Canadian lifestyle and the unavoidable realities they were all born into. A capsule description of this "taking part" activity that is supervised by their chief requires each participant to find and maintain full employment and to participate in a co-op venture with a portion of their earnings. There are many other conditions for membership in this select group that have not been made an issue. They are concerned with the education and training of their young people, with a view to them being prepared to take part in this new venture in a few short years, when they will be ready to take an active part. These people have become shareholder-owners of several thriving business ventures in only a few years, and they continue to move forward at an amazing pace. They are constantly attempting to recruit newcomers from tribe members in their general area, but they have a hard set of standards that must be met by any new member.

The co-op activities by this group of people are not entirely in keeping with the political views of many of our current population; however, they must be recognized as being a long way better than the positions taken by most of their contemporaries across our nation. I have recently heard of some positive actions among other groups of natives in the LaRonge area of Saskatchewan and in the Blood tribal area of Alberta. A number of the natives in these areas have been successful with ventures similar to the South Okanagan experiences.

These bold advances clearly show that the only workable and valid solutions up to this time have come from inside the native communities. We are all subject to the basic fact of life that if something has no direct cost to us then it also has a diminished value. Handouts have only a short-term benefit; however, they do serve well to reinforce a feeling of dependency and entitlement.

Tragically, these three splinter groups of natives are experiencing negative input from kin and countrymen who have chosen to remain dependent on the native reserve system. This adds to the reluctance of many others to attempt such a move or to join in the successes experienced by these people. A small portion of the many billions of dollars presently being spent on welfare-like programs for our reserve-dwelling natives should be channeled toward assistance to and recognition of these brave people who have chosen to break away from their present dead end existence and take part in the modern world.

A strange fact of these effective and ambitious native actions is that almost no information has been put forward about these experiments to the general Canadian population and, more importantly, to the many other native tribes across the nation. It seems that the general public and the natives across Canada are being kept in the dark about the success of these determined and ambitious people. Could it be that the propagation of such information would be contrary and embarrassing to the established plans and programs set out for our native populations? Would it be politically incorrect to spread the word about programs that have been planned and implemented wholly from within the native communities and that have been embarrassingly successful?

Whatever the answers are to these questions, the ambitious people participating in these ventures should be supported and congratulated for their courage, strength, and ambition. After 300 or more years of experiments and the expenditures of untold billions of dollars, the only successful solution to the native situation has come from among themselves. Congratulations to all those who have taken part in these difficult departures from what has become the norm for many of these people.

The obvious lack of information being made available to the other native people and the general Canadian population is somewhat puzzling to those of us who have given it some thought. This willful lack of the spread of good information will likely be followed by an effort to discredit the hard-working natives who have embarked on these difficult but effective ventures. Those among us who make it their business to embellish the unworkable situations of our modern natives will be faced with the need for sabotage and dis-information programs directed toward these hard-working natives to support the long established but unsuccessful native programs of the past 300 years. The native situation has become almost an industry for those who pretend to assist the native people and these people will not want to see their loyal subjects wandering off into greener pastures.

The actions by these few natives are, perhaps, an example of what the people who began the reserve systems in Canada had in their minds at the outset. Those people had only their own life experiences to work with when they were faced with finding a solution for the natives; they were ambitious and willing people or they would not have made their way to Canada and, therefore, they could not imagine the reserve solution as anything other than temporary. These people could see nothing but opportunities in the future of their adopted country. How could they possibly have envisioned the reserve system still in existence after all these years? These early Canadians could not visualize or understand the fear of change and the negative attitude of the natives; they could only see the multitude of opportunities before them.

Chapter 45
Good Intentions Gone Bad

Much has been observed and recorded about the preferential or at the least specialized treatment of native Canadians in their dealings with our courts and many other aspects of daily life in this country. There are few examples where this course of action has been beneficial to the majority of natives in any way. Many natives accused of crimes have been acquitted because of the preferential and specialized treatment allowed them in the courts, but the overall effect of this consideration has not been positive for these people. In most cases, it is seen by the natives as exactly what it has been: a reward for unacceptable behaviour and a worsening of their overall situation.

A recent story in the newspapers tells of a pedestrian fatality where a sixty-six-year-old woman was struck in a crosswalk in an interior British Columbia city. The driver was a native man who had a criminal driving record accumulated over the past thirty years. He had never held a valid and permanent driver's license. He was convicted at trial and sentenced to six months in jail. This sentence is quite amazing when one considers the fact of death for his victim. The native man appealed on the grounds that the judge had not properly considered his aboriginal background. British Columbia Supreme Court Justice Alison Beames agreed and placed the man on a seven-month suspended sentence. She stated that this criminal's decision to drive was linked to his circumstances as an aboriginal person. The news story made no mention of the reaction of the family of the dead woman. Had the situation been reversed, there may well have been street demonstrations.

A well-documented story from many years ago in the central Cariboo region is about two young members of the Royal Canadian Mounted Police accused of murder in the death of a native man after a drunken vehicle incident. The wife of the dead man began this vicious conspiracy on the spur of the moment, and she immediately received detailed backup for every aspect of her fabricated story from a number of others in her native community. The two policemen went through hell on Earth at two coroners' inquests, where all these native witnesses gave sworn evidence that they had seen extreme violence which, years later, was found to have not occurred. The juries at both inquests ruled that there was no conclusive evidence to support the alleged criminal assaults the witnesses tried to describe to them.

Obviously, their fabricated stories could not withstand the test of probabilities and common sense that the juries applied. The principal accuser, the wife of the dead man, made a confession on her deathbed about six years later that the entire story had been lies and, therefore, perjury. The examination of the transcripts from the coroners' inquests would have provided detailed evidence of perjury by all these witnesses, yet there was no action instigated against the many natives involved.

The police recommended charges; however, such action must be cleared by our well-educated crown lawyers and these people found no necessity for charges against these aboriginals. The most senior people in our justice system have convinced themselves that preferential treatment of native offenders is appreciated by these people; however, having observed this conduct over many years, I am convinced that the native people look on it only as a demonstration of weakness.

The many misguided witnesses who supported the lies of this woman are now parents, grandparents, and great-grandparents. All we as the dominant society can hope for is that something will have brought about a change of attitude among the descendants of these people, although that possibility seems remote. The main and original accuser of these two policemen was the wife of the native man who was fatally injured when she backed over him with their truck.

In her deathbed confession, this woman also told of having shot and killed another native woman some years before the incident with the two policemen. The murder was committed on her isolated home reserve during a drunken potlatch. She also told of having shot ranchers' cattle in her home area, mainly for recreational or hatred purposes. She had given evidence after the murder of this woman on her reserve that she had seen a young native man fire the killing shots. He was charged with murder and convicted, mainly by her sworn testimony, and sentenced to life. He was still in prison when her confession became known. He was immediately released and was, no doubt, the recipient of a large cash payment that could not possibly make up for his many years in prison during the prime of his life.

The modern tendency to lay the fault for most of the negative activities by natives on the residential school system does not fit in this case. The main witness in this tragedy of lies had somehow evaded the compulsory schooling; she had never attended one of these places.

The failure by our justice system to take action on the abundant perjury offences in this case may have contributed to the recent willingness of four native witnesses to lie about the conduct of a former teacher at a Burns Lake, British Columbia, residential school. The willingness of our justice system to accept information from native witnesses without question contributed to the apparent false accusations against this man. When the proper questions and inquiries were finally undertaken, investigators learned that one of the four witnesses had never even attended the school involved, though her story indicated she was a student there at the time of the accusations. From that point onward, the case fell apart, but the damage to the man's reputation will never be corrected. The actions, if any, which will be taken, or not taken, against these witnesses should be of interest to all of us; the many examples of inaction by our justice system leaves little doubt about how this incident will be dealt with.

There are many valid reasons for the Canadian prison population being severely over-represented by native people. In spite of the preferential and overly patient treatment by the courts, the natives of all the areas I was familiar with in my lifetime were the most identifiable group before the courts. The attitude among these people and the extreme abuse of alcohol and other mind-altering substances are the primary reasons; however, there is an obvious lack of motivation to deal with, or to even talk about, this fact in our present society. The native attitude about life in general is also a strong contributing factor in their lawlessness.

In more recent times, abuse of illicit drugs has loomed large among young natives and has now possibly overtaken alcohol as the most abused substance among these people. The obviously unmotivated conduct on the reserves contributes to this tragic trend. How could a young person growing up on a reserve have any chance of developing a positive attitude about life when they are faced with neglect and abuse every day of their formative years?

The natives are by far the leaders in police statistics when alcohol- or drug-related crimes are examined. These people seem to have no will or ability to deal with the negative effects of either of these substances. The time is now to look at the condition of the individual at the time of their crime rather than simply counting the number of natives in relation to the overall numbers in our courts and prisons. There is no hope for a lesser count of natives in the prisoner docket without significant effort to alter the overall attitude and to reduce the use and abuse of alcohol and drugs among these people. These efforts, to have any positive effect whatsoever, must come from among the natives themselves and will require a huge change in the overall attitude among these people.

The offences being tried by our courts are not limited to public intoxication; alcohol and drugs are a significant contributing factor in many crimes by natives or any other citizens. A thorough examination of police statistics and reports clearly shows the relationship between crime and intoxication, including all crimes, from homicide to minor theft, regardless of the racial or ethnic backgrounds of the offenders. There is no doubt that if accurate and truthful statistics were gathered they would clearly show the extremely high rate of intoxication in native as in all offenders before, during, and after their criminal acts.

Chapter 46
Billions of Dollars

Recently, our prime minister, Steven Harper, appeared at a public venue and delivered an apology to the native Indian population of our nation for the suggested evils done by the residential school system. The prime minister announced at the same meeting that our federal government is preparing to deliver another $1.9 billion into the incompetent hands of the natives so they can be totally in control of their education systems.

The history of native misuse of money seems to have no effect on the next government scheme that allows this grand tradition to continue on a larger scale after each previous financial disaster. This was a low point in the history of our nation and it will haunt us for generations. Hopefully, the apology soothed some of the ill feelings among some of the native population, but this is unlikely and contrary to the history of the entire native situation.

Prior to the delivery of another apology, there should have been a great deal of research into the motivation of our leaders of those times, the vital need for this long-ago attempt at education, and, more importantly, the general improvement of the native way of life. The government officials of those times must have witnessed or been informed of many events among the natives that influenced them deeply and brought about the establishment of the schools. There are written records of this facet of our history that should be looked at with a view of understanding the entire message, not only the points that can be used against these early people. The situation on reserves across the country must have been far worse than what we see today to bring our government authorities to the point where they authorized and funded the residential schools.

In the Western world, the family unit has always been nearly sacred; therefore, there must have been some truly mind boggling situations among the majority of the native population for our leaders to sanction such a drastic move. There can be no doubt that our selected leaders of that time looked for every possible way to bring education to the native children but finally came to the conclusion that the residential schools, while far from ideal, would be the most viable solution. Today, we all join together to condemn those hard-working and dedicated people who were faced with truly unbelievable situations on an almost daily basis.

Sir John A. MacDonald was the Canadian prime minister at the time the schools became a reality. A recent news article followed the grand tradition of generous criticism of any and all who were involved in trying to deal with the Canadian natives and their problems of those times. Some quotes credited to Sir John A. MacDonald in that article do truly sound racist and uncaring in the proper English of today; however, some thought should be given to the times he lived in and the frustration that must have reigned supreme for those charged with attempting to do something for the Canadian natives. With the overall mindsets displayed by the people who are so vociferous about this aspect of our history, we can be sure that many of the words and phrases that have been credited to our leaders of those times have been carefully selected and edited to fit into the purposes of these misinformed people. Those of us who are truly embarrassed about such language should give some thought to what we would be saying today if our leaders in those times had just ignored the native situation and left it to nature. Such a course of action would not have been open for anyone in those times, because every one of the new Canadians had a deep understanding of the laws of nature and the immense potential for a cruel end for anyone who was totally reliant on it. We should try to find some motivation to be less critical of the early arrivals and those they chose to be their leaders.

These people were quite obviously not the totally evil bastards being pictured to our students in our schools today. If the evil among our leaders and the general population portrayed in modern school lessons was half as vicious and cruel as our students are led to believe, the native problems of today would not likely exist. If Sir John A. MacDonald had been as hateful and as single minded as he is portrayed, he could quite simply have found reason to declare war on the natives.

Modern school lessons indicate that the vast majority of the citizens of those times would have supported such an act, yet in spite of all these "hard facts" being presented to the students, this did not happen. This non-happening should require some changes to the modern attitude so clearly displayed in our schools; however, I suspect that this uncomfortable suggestion will have to be simply swept under the well-used carpet of our modern thinkers and doers. For those who find it difficult to believe that such things are being taught in our modern schools, may I refer you to the grade ten course of studies in the subject known as Social Studies, in British Columbia schools.

Chapter 47
Conclusion

I have frequently talked of politically correct conduct in this book; therefore, I am closing with the best definition of this thing that I have heard. "Political correctness is the belief among many that it is possible to pick up a turd by the clean end."

The human populations of our world are made up of a fascinating variety of people who each have their place in history. There have always been and will continue to be a mixture that defies definition or cataloguing or any hard and fast placements by cultures or customs. There have always been individuals, couples, families, clans, tribes, and groups, right up to nations and continents, where a great variety of people have existed forever. The strengths or weaknesses of them all have been equally influential contributors in all these situations.

The inherent assumption among all of humanity that there is a supreme being and that we are all entitled to life everlasting has resulted in a great assortment of religious beliefs, which has brought about unending conflict among the many various beliefs and branches of these dedicated believers. All these belief patterns can be cited for achievements and failures; however, some stand out as being exceptional in both or one of these manmade measures. If there is a place on this Earth for political correctness, it is in looking at these religion-based aspects of human history and behaviour. Anyone who attempts to give credit or criticism to any of these belief patterns will be on thin ice, as they will be unable to sort the "fly shit from the pepper."

Charles Scheideman

The practice of overstating or embellishing the facts or accomplishments of any group or race of people leads to errors and omissions that only add to the already confusing history of humanity. These differences of opinion or thought patterns about religious beliefs have added to the patterns of conflict, hate, and war.

We can all point out accomplishments or failures by any branch of humanity, from individuals to entire races, but such comparisons or examples do little for anyone. We should all struggle with the difficult task of "telling it as it is" rather than the way we "wish it was" or the way we would "like it to be." The primary purpose of this book is not to elevate or to diminish the abilities or accomplishments of any individual or race of humanity. Hopefully, it will promote better understanding among some or many of us, to the extent that we look beyond the obvious measures we all apply when we compare among us. The exaggeration or diminishment of the accomplishments, failures, or abilities of any of us can only lead to inaccurate conclusions and more confusion. Let us all try our best to "tell it as it is," to the best of our abilities and understanding. The powerful human desire to "tell things as we wish they were" or "as we would like things to be" must be avoided. The disasters created by this weakness are abundantly displayed in the native situations across this country.